TOKENS

A Play on the Plague

by David Schein

with Music composed & arranged by
Candace Natvig English & David Schein

Fomite
Burlington, VT

Cover image from original production poster by Jen-Ann Kirchmeier
Text and lyrics David Schein, music compositions and arrangements from the original production
Candace Natvig English and David Schein

For permission for professional or amateur production, public readings or any other performance of TOKENS: A Play on the Plague contact David Schein at davidschein.net.

To obtain a score and arrangements of the music and permissions to use the music
contact Candace Natvig English at candacenatvigenglish.com.

ISBN-13: 978-1-959984-26-9
Library of Congress Control Number: 2023941227

Fomite
58 Peru Street
Burlington, VT 05401
www.fomitepress.com
08-11-2023

Tokens: The Original Production

TOKENS was originally produced by the Blake Street Hawkeyes, Mixed Bag Productions & Whoopi Goldberg in association with Theater Artaud.

TOKENS ran for six weeks from May 16th, 1985 to June 30th, 1985 at Theater Artaud in San Francisco. This was at a time when a mysterious and fatal disease was wreaking havoc in San Francisco; known then as "Gay Cancer," it was soon to be called AIDS (Auto Immune Deficiency Syndrome) and now, HIV (Human Immunodeficiency Virus). Only later, after TOKENS was produced, was the transmission vector of the disease identified. The similarities of the HIV pandemic to the Great Plague of London—the mystery of transmission, the pursuit of fatuous and real treatments, the heroism and charlatanism it brought out in the population and governing institutions—was prescient, as it is again in the time of Covid. At that time of panic (1985) the Bay Area's performing arts community, reeling from the crisis, came together to make TOKENS a devastating act of catharsis in the theater.

This book is dedicated to those in the cast who have since died from complications from HIV/AIDS.

Peter Collins
Paul Cyr
Peter David Heth
Chuck Hilbert
W.B. Higgs
Jack Stellman
Dan Turner
and Jim Tyler

The original cast and credits are as follows:

SCRIPT AND MUSIC

Script: David Schein
Music: composed and arranged by Candace Natvig English and David Schein

DIRECTION AND DESIGN

Director: Bob Ernst
Musical Director: Candace Natvig English
Choreography: John LeFan and Freddie Long
Production Design, Sets & Costumes: Peter David Heth
Lighting Design: Brian Mulhern
Makeup: Chuck Hilburt

PRINCIPALS

Guard: Don Hart
Dolphin: Chuck Hilbert
Mort: Mark Gordon
Euwa: Karen Hott
Weldon: Michael Charnes
Doctor: Alan Phillips
Mumm: Christin Haupert
Dunn: Gilberto Sanchez
Willie: Kris LeFan
Phoebe: Astrid Harper
Bridget: Alex Martin
Dead-Carter #1: James Tyler
Dead-Carter #2: Claudia Oehrle
Watchman: Bob Taxin

Nurse: Freddie Long
Piper: Lynn Grasberg

THE CITIZENS

Ben Bacot, Victoria Bogart, Chelley BonDurant, Kimberly Brown (Alto Horn), Sarah Bryant, Peter Collins, Paul Cyr, LuAnne Daly, Paul Dawson, Sheila Edwards-May, Ann Elliott, Susan Engbrecht, Kim Fowler, Mary Alice Fry, Gigi Gamble, Laurie Glenn, W.B. Higgs (Penny Whistle), Laura Hitt, Hillary Hurst (Field Drum, Jenny Klion, Dorothy Lefkovits, John LeFan, Amy Ludwig (Penny Whistle), Jan Mauro, Sharon McGowan ,Connie Moomey, Michael O'Brien, Cathleen O'Connell (Irish Harp), Joye Peters, Kristina Peterson, Delilah Raybee, Elizabeth Raybee, Sharon Silverglate, Jack Stellman, Kym Trippsmith, Sonia Turanski, Dan Turner, Penny Wallace, Laura Washington, James Williams, Kari Wishingrad

MUSICIANS

Piper: Lynn Grasberg
Sackbut: John English
Violins: Candace Natvig English & Caitlin Reed

OFFICIALS

Chris Brophy, PJ Flowers, Robbyn Gianattasio, Kim Santa, Arnold Schein, Florence Schein

PRODUCTION STAFF

Production Stage Manager: Elizabeth Spicuzza
Technical Director: Steve Clifford

Assistant Director: Paul Codiga
Operator: Victor Schneider

TOKENS Background

London suffered five epidemics of bubonic plague in the 17th Century. "The Great Plague of 1665 was by far the worst, killing an estimated 120,000 people out of a population of 500,000. It was called the "Poor's' Plague," since anyone with means fled the town as the death toll mounted.

The first deaths were reported in April, south of the city walls. By June, the plague had entered the city, and the King and the Court had fled. In September, when TOKENS takes place, it was at its peak, with 9,000 deaths a week, and all the resources of the city were taxed by the insurmountable problem of how to bury the dead. The practice of quarantining plague victims and shutting them up in their houses dates from the Plague of 1641. Searchers and Examiners were hired by the parishes to find those with signs of the plague upon them. These were called "Tokens of the Plague," carbuncles and pustules that would appear on the bodies of the infected. Everyone, sick or not, who resided with a plague victim was locked in their house for forty days. A red cross was painted on the door of the house, with the words, "Lord have mercy on us." A Watchman was appointed to guard the door and to provide food and drink for the inhabitants of the quarantined house. The job of Nurse, women who were placed in the house to "care" for the sick, often fell to the most desperate women of the town. The record of their plundering, and even of murdering their victims, are legion. This intended "remedy" of quarantine served to kill thousands of people.

Plague deaths started declining in October of 1665. By February 1666, the King and the Court felt safe enough to return to London, while people continued to die of the plague up until

September 1666, when the Great Fire devastated most of the old city. London was rebuilt with brick and stone. Sewage was drained into the Thames, and the breeding places of rats, whose fleas are the carriers of bubonic plague, were inadvertently wiped out. One of the most striking things about such epidemics as the Black Death and the Great Plague is that, in those times, no one knew that the real reason for such devastation was a flea. Whether it was the licentiousness of the Court, God's vengeance, witchcraft, poor hygiene, foul vapors or a plot of the Dutch – it was all up to conjecture, much as it was in 1985, when TOKENS was produced; a new, mysterious and deadly disease was sweeping the globe and no one knew the source.

The Setting of TOKENS

TOKENS takes place on September 8, 1665, by all accounts the worst day of the worst week of The Great Plague of London. Almost ten thousand people died that week and the systems devised by the Lord Mayor for keeping order and for disposing of the corpses had broken down. The streets of London were full of homeless desperate people and rotting corpses.

The Cast

THE PRINCIPALS

DOLPHIN
A religious fanatic, representative of a dissenting faction of Puritans who thought the plague was divine retribution for the relaxation of pubic mores that accompanied the Stuart Restoration. Dedicated to burying the dead and conducting illegal funerals, DOLPHIN is a fatalist who believes that Gawd is using the plague to wipe the world free of sin.

EUWA
In her early thirties, common-law wife of MORT, mother of WILLIE, granddaughter of

WELDON, daughter of DUNN and MUMM. She's tough but she cracks when WILLIE dies and only regains herself after she lets go of his corpse. EUWA has a birthmark on her neck and chin which GUARDS mistake for a sign of the plague.

WELDON
An old man in his seventies, father of MUMM. He's lived through five epidemics. Now, as TOKENS opens, he has the plague again, but he's covering up his "tokens" and not telling anyone. He is very careful not to touch anyone and he doesn't let anybody touch him. Though ill himself, he tries to drive MORT off when MORT is brought home sick by THE GUARDS.

DUNN
A man in his fifties, husband of MUMM, father of EUWA. He too becomes ill. When he breaks out with the tokens, the fatal manifestation of the plague, he succumbs serenely after requesting that his family and friends dance on his grave.

MORT
EUWA'S man, in his thirties.

WILLIE
EUWA'S young son. He dies and EUWA refuses to let his corpse be buried.

DEAD-CARTER 1
A DEAD-CARTER who collects the corpses and takes them to THE PIT. He/She dies.

DEAD-CARTER 2
DEAD-CARTER 1's partner.

GUARD
A corrupt official. He keeps THE GATE, inspects the certificates of health, rounds up sick people and tries in vain to keep order. Also works in cahoots with THE NURSE and THE WATCHMAN, stealing the possessions of the quarantined plague victims.

THE DOCTOR
A man or woman. Always wears a mask and protective clothing.

NURSE
A woman in her fifties, a drunkard and a thief. She tries to suffocate EUWA and steal the DUNN's possessions.

WATCHMAN
The GUARD's underling, posted to watch the DUNN's quarantined house. He is the NURSE's accomplice in thievery and possibly much worse.

PIPER
Personification of the legendary "plague piper" who passes out drunk, is assumed dead and is buried in THE PIT. They awaken from their drunken stupor and arise from amidst the corpses playing their pipes. Also is one of the musicians.

THE CITIZENS
MUSICIANS
They provide accompaniment for the musical numbers and illustrate transitions and dramatic action with their instruments. They are an integral part of the CITIZENRY. Their characters are those of street musicians.

CHORUS — The FERVENT
Followers of DOLPHIN. Many of them have lost their families and have "gone demented".

Others are Puritans like DOLPHIN. They work in THE PIT, bury the dead, hold funerals and are very much in DOLPHIN's sway.

CHORUS — The Street People
Those who have no place to go but the street. Many of them have escaped from quarantined houses. Others have been caught in The City and can't get a Bill of Health permitting them to leave. Some are sick, some are not. Many die during the show. Often their ranks are swollen by all the other CITIZENS.

THE DEAD
They fall often during the play. Eventually, they are loaded onto the dead-cart and taken to THE PIT. Some are dummies. All are dead. If the cast is small, they can reappear as other living souls.

> NOTE: *Every member of the CITIZENS should choose a name and devise a history under the guidance of the director. THE CITIZENS are the living solution in which all the action of the play is suspended.*

OFFICIALS
THE OFFICIALS move THE AUDIENCE and sometimes THE CITIZENS. They have wooden staffs, help guard THE GATE, enforce the regulations and act as ushers. Non-singing parts.

AUDIENCE
THE AUDIENCE is a vital part of TOKENS. They comprise, with THE CITIZENS, the crowds of London at the beginning and the end of the play and at all transitions when they move with the cast. They are visitors to The City who have been permitted to enter only because they are holding Bills of Health. It is very important that they are often in the middle of the action as well as outside of it.

Notes on the Set and Staging of TOKENS

The stage directions in this script are for an environmental staging using up to four different areas. The OFFICIALS guide the AUDIENCE from area to area with their sticks.

OUTSIDE THE GATE: This is where the audience buys their tickets, receives their Certificates of Health and waits for THE GATE to open. Through THE GATE are visible THE CITIZENS and THE SQUARE INSIDE THE GATE.

THE SQUARE INSIDE THE GATE: A large square facing THE GATE inside the walls of the city. One side is bordered with a multi-level platform at least four feet high with broad steps leading up to it. A street leads from THE SQUARE INSIDE THE GATE to the DUNN's HOUSE.

THE STREET OUSIDE THE DUNN's HOUSE: Connects THE SQUARE with THE PIT. It is bordered on one side by a hillock and on the other side by the DUNN's HOUSE. The DUNN's HOUSE is open to THE AUDIENCE who are seated on risers that command a view of the whole area. THE DUNN's HOUSE has an upstairs with a window on the street. Most entrances and exits are up and down a ladder from this window.

THE PIT: Its entrance is obscured from THE STREET OUTSIDE THE PIT by a bridge. It is an amphitheater looking down on a large hole filled with THE DEAD.

The above environmental staging is the ideal based on the original production at Theater Artaud, written for the (then) open space of Theater Artaud. Those who wish to stage TOKENS in proscenium, three-quarters, in-the-round or outdoors, please be inventive. The original staging in the vast regions of Theater Artaud, managed to use three of the four suggested areas.

The author would like to thank Steve Clifford, Candace Natvig English, Robert Ernst, Whoopi Goldberg, John LeFan, Freddie Long, Lizzie Spicuzza and the entire cast and crew of TOKENS. Without their belief and collective inspiration the integration of music, dance and theater that made TOKENS utterly unique could never have occurred.

The inclusion of illustrations in this script was made possible by a grant from the Vermont Council on the Arts.

TOKENS

A Play on the Plague

SCENE 1

*(AUDIENCE waits outside THE GATE. They buy tickets which are Certificates
of Health, permitting them to enter the city. Through THE GATE can be seen the
CITIZENS who slowly fill THE SQUARE inside THE GATE. They are a rowdy, rag
taggle lot, many of whom are ill. OFFICIALS guard THE GATE, keeping AUDIENCE
from getting in and the CITIZENS from getting out. High up on a catwalk above
THE GATE, walks GUARD. THE MUSICIANS play a folk-tune (O'Keefe's Slide). A
DRUMMER appears on THE GATE with GUARD. Drumroll)*

GUARD

(singing/intoning)

Know yee…that the Lord Mayor decrees…that all those infected by the Plague…

CITIZENS

Not me, not me!

GUARD

…be hunted out and shut up in their houses. That access and egress to such infected houses be denied…

CITIZENS

Be defied!

GUARD

…that two watchmen be appointed, one by day and one by night to provide the necessities within, that searchers…

CITIZENS

VULTURES!

GUARD

…be named to search out the dead, that surgeons name the cause of death…

CITIZENS

…is the surgeons. Quack, quack, quack, quack…

GUARD

…that nurses…

CITIZENS

MURDERESSES!

GUARD

…keep the living and stay in the houses…

CITIZENS

…till they're dead and the last bed is sold.

GUARD

…for forty days from the last sign of the Plague. That every house visited be marked by a red cross of a foot long, and with these words: "Lord have mercy on us."

CITIZENS

Lord have mercy on us. (*They sing this with GUARD*)

GUARD

TO HELL WITH YOU!

CITIZENS

TO HELL WITH YOU!!

GUARD

All plays, public feastings, *funerals*, and public drunkenness…are prohibited.

CITIZENS

What about me? What about me? What about me? What about…?

SCENE 2

GUARD

Get ready. Out of the way. Watch the mob.

(*THE GATE opens. OFFICIALS guide AUDIENCE through THE GATE, while preventing THE CITIZENS and THE PRINCIPALS from escaping. AUDIENCE enters into a mob of singing dancing CITIZENS and PRINCIPALS in THE SQUARE.*)

If You're Going To London
(Song)

ALL

If you're going to London don't come,
don't come in, don't come in.
If you've left your wife and family in London,
they're done in, they're done in.
Get another wife and family.
Get another life while you've still got one.
They're done in, done in London.
Take a little country air.
Friend, be a fair-weather friend, fair-weather friend.
Farewell or fare thee well, if by friends or family infected.
Don't come in, don't come in…

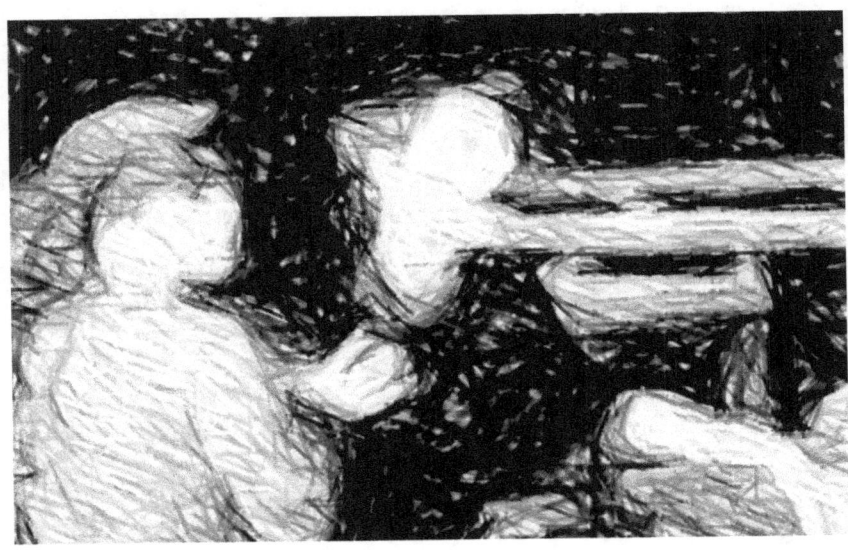

If you're coming from London, go back in,
You're done in, you're done in, you're done in.
Better dig your grave in London
while you still can find some room for a grave.
Go, go back to dig your gra-hey-hey-ave
in Lon…don…don go the bells
in Lon…don...don go the bells.

Un-done, un-done, un-done,
Undone, undone, undone…

I'm done, I'm done, I'm done in London town
I'm plum undone.
I wanna die in the country air alone,
not in a pit in a town.
Not in a pit, not in a pit,
not in a pit in a town…

*(AUDIENCE enters into the flux of the singing and dancing crowd. From a
different direction THE FERVENT enter in a funeral procession. They bear a
small casket containing the body of a child and cut through the mob, which
now contains AUDIENCE.*

The Fervent's Dirge
(Song)

FERVENT

Gawd has taken another soul.
Glory be to Gawd.

This little child has now grown cold.
Come and praise His Name.

He couldn't wait till she got cold.
His is our One Path.

He needed for to take his toll.
Let us give Him thanks.

For keeping us in his control.
Gawd is glorious.

(THE FERVENT's funeral procession, led by the SACKBUT PLAYER, threads through the crowd (consisting of AUDIENCE and the singing/ dancing CITIZENS. The preacher DOLPHIN mounts the stairs and begin his rant to the crowd. OFFICIALS and the CITIZENS guide AUDIENCE into the center of the action. GUARDS close THE GATE. All are now inside the City.)

DOLPHIN

And do you wonder from whence comes
this terrible visitation swift unto London?
Do you lament the loss of loved ones
cry out like Christ on the cross, crucified,
"Oh Lord, why has though forsaken me?"
The Lord has not forsaken thee.
Thou has forsaken him and he is remembering thee.
Now his broom sweeps London clean with fever
casting out the unbeliever.

(In the distance another funeral procession can be heard approaching. The DUNNS and some friends are burying the late Mrs. Mortibrew.)

Isn't It Grand" (trad.)
(Song)
DUNNS & CITIZENS

Look at the Preacher.
Bloody big hypocrite.
Isn't it grand, boys.
To be bloody well dead?
Let's not have a sniffle
Let's have a bloody good cry.
Always remember the longer you live
The sooner you'll bloody well die.

DOLPHIN

Thou has forsaken him and he is remembering thee.

There is no escape, no turning back, no hope for salvation now.

You, who are saved so suddenly now,

you who confess that you have feasted with the dog on your own vomit

and returned with the sow to the wallowing of the mires

Oh, tardy turncoats, you are doomed, DOOMED!

Gawd would sooner have you dead than have you profess convenient faith,

Sooner burn the seeds of equivocation than have them sprout in wicked soil again.

IT IS TOO LATE FOR YOU!

DUNNS/CITIZENS
(Song)

Look at the doctors

Bloody great charlatans.

Isn't it grand, boys

To be bloody well dead?

Let's not have sniffle, etc...

(The funeral procession enters THE SQUARE, let by the fiddlers. The CITIZENS join in their wake. The procession threads through the crowd up onto a platform, fronted by steps. Striving to regain the crowd's attention, DOLPHIN mounts the platform with the DUNNS. He Is being drowned out.)

The funeral procession takes over "If You're Going to London," which turns into "Isn't It Grand Boys," and is sung by all. DOLPHIN has to fight to be heard, but his voice is huge.)

DOLPHIN

Sear us sire
with your fire.
Take us hard.
Let no man stay
no stained innocence remain.

Lord, scourge London
with thy fever,
that we may fear
thy whip forever.
Let fear's river
drown thy anger.

Lord, take London
from within.
Let sin bloom roses
on her skin
till none remain
to sin again.

DUNNS & CITIZENS
(Song)

Look at the body
All bloody withered.
Isn't it grand, boys…etc.

(MORT is getting an attack of the chills. He is stumbling and weaving about and as the FERVENT's funeral begins to separate from the DUNN's funeral and AUDIENCE, MORT drops the corner of the coffin he's carrying. It tumbles, spills open, and the swollen, disfigured corpse of Mrs. Mortibrew, a dummy, rolls out. Screams from ALL. OFFICIALS and GUARD back AUDIENCE away from the body. MORT's teeth are chattering loudly. He stumbles, then falls on top of the corpse. A disconcerted EUWA and WELDON pull him up to his feet.)

SCENE 3

EUWA

Shhh. He's fine he didn't sleep last night, that's all.

GUARD

Get a doctor.

MORT

I've got the chills.

WELDON

Shut up, they'll lock us up if they…

GUARD

Do you know this man?

WELDON

Never seen him before in me…

                              EUWA

He's my man.

                    (Simultaneous)

                              MUMM

He's her man.

                              GUARD

These funerals are against the regulations.

                              MUMM

Before she died she asked for a wake.

          (MORT'S teeth chatter audibly. Can be played by bones.)

                              GUARD

This man is ill. Where's the examiner?

                              MORT

I am fuh…FINE!

          (MORT runs away into THE SQUARE.)

          (GUARD and WATCHMAN chase MORT through the crowd and disappear.)

                              EUWA

Did you feel him? Hot as a fish in a baking dish. We've got to find him. We've got to get him
home and call the doctor.

WELDON

NO! If they find out that he's one of us they'll lock us in the house with him for forty bleedin' days and he'll infect the lot of us.

EUWA

Christ, Gramps…he's me man. We can't just leave him to die in the streets or be dragged off to the pest-house.

WELDON

Look, I've lived through five plagues and it's like this. It's either let him go or we'll get it. Leave him and save ourselves or go the Christian way and risk it. Besides he never earned his keep.

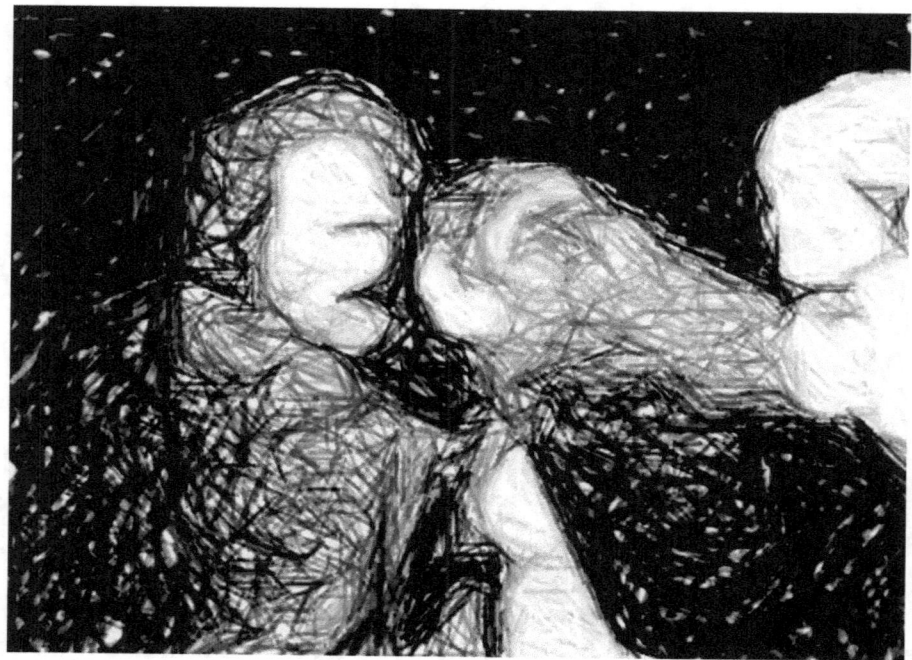

MUMM

Shut up, Dad. Of course we'll help him, Euwa. He's one of the family and we've got to stick by him. What do you say Dad?

DUNN

I'll see it done.

MUMM

What?

DUNN

I don't want to die. But…I've lived a good life, but, oh, I don't know. Either way, leave him and save ourselves, or go the Christian way and we'll all fall sick and find relief in heaven.

EUWA

Look, I'm after him.

WELDON

That's good, darlin. Love'll have us all dead.

EUWA

I will bring him home.

WILLIE

But Gramps, he's one of the family now. We've got to stick by him.

WELDON

Well, don't be touchin' or kissin' on him then. He's a ghost already by the looks of it.

MUMM

We'll make up a room for him. A special room.

EUWA

I'm gone.

(She threads her way through the crowd. DOLPHIN has been listening to the DUNNS.)

WILLIE

But what about Mrs. Mortibrew? We were having such a jolly wake.

DOLPHIN

It is to no avail you Gawdless animals. You have fornicated licentiously, and this is thy reward. Join us now and…

WELDON

SHUT YER BLEEDIN' 'OLE, YOU FUCKIN' WITCH!!

(THE DUNNS restrain WELDON who is going for DOLPHIN's throat.)

(GUARD and WATCHMAN return without MORT.)

DUNN

I suppose we ought to be going.

GUARD

Right. Break up these funerals. Leave the bodies for the dead carts. How many times do we have to tell you? It is illegal to congregate in public, even for a funeral. You are all risking infection. It's all the same to the dead whether you pray at home or accompany them to the Pit. Their soul is departed, and all that's left is rotted meat. SO, DEPART! GO HOME!

DOLPHIN

HEED HIM NOT! Congregate! Pray for forgiveness! Shrive each other's souls. Make funerals. He is the barking jackal of a swinish court, the cackling jay of a befouled nest of corruption. The Queen is a Papist. The King is…

GUARD

HOLD YER TONGUE!

(GUARD hits DOLPHIN on the head with the end of his pike, stunning him.)

DOLPHIN

Gawd will punish you.

(DOLPHIN spits in GUARD's face. He runs off as WATCHMAN runs in.)

GUARD

After him! (WATCHMAN runs after DOLPHIN.) Disperse!

WELDON

Take the kids. We'll meet at home.

MUMM

Gawd willing.

WELDON

Gawd has nothing to do with it.

(MUMM, DUNN, WELDON and the KIDS leave THE SQUARE. The dead cart parts the crowd.)

SCENE 4

Dead-Carter's Call: Bring Out Yer Bodies (1)
(Song)

(The DEAD-CARTERS approach, pulling their cart into THE SQUARE. A couple of bodies are on the cart.

DEAD-CARTERs (*singing*)

Bring out your bodies
Bring out your deh-heh-hed, deh-heh-heh-heh-hed.

(*They look at the available bodies in THE SQUARE.*)

DEAD-CARTER 1

Which one you say?

DEAD-CARTER 2

That one. Well, I'll be a Christmas goose. I knew that one. 'E used to have a fine baritone voice.

DEAD-CARTER 1

That one?

DEAD-CARTER 2

No, not that one. That othah one over there, next to the fat one.

DEAD-CARTER 1

Oh Lawd, not anothah fat one.

DEAD-CARTER 2

She's not as bad as that othah one. I nearly broke my back on that one.

(*They are loading the bodies onto the cart.*)

DEAD-CARTER 1

Them fat ones aren't half so bad as those awful sof' ones.

DEAD-CARTER 2

Them sof' ones will drive you off your nut.

DEAD-CARTER 1

You can't tell if they're on or off the cart.

DEAD-CARTER 2

You don't know if you've got 'old of them or not.

DEAD-CARTER 1

And the foul stench of 'em. It could drive a man to drink.

DEAD-CARTER 2

It's driving me there right now.

(DEAD-CARTER 2 produces a bottle. They swig on it.)

DEAD-CARTER 1

'Tis better to be driven to drink than to 'ave to walk to it.

DEAD-CARTER 2

Here's to the light ones.

DEAD-CARTER 1

To the skinny ones.

DEAD-CARTER 2

To the lovely little bitty ones, Gawd rest their souls.

DEAD-CARTER 1

There aren't many of them left.

DEAD-CARTER 2

No, they're all gone.

(They are hefting huge Mrs. Mortibrew onto the cart.)

DEAD-CARTER 1

Plenty of large ones though.

DEAD-CARTER 2

Don't tell my back that.

DEAD-CARTER 1

It's not fair. They should stay alive, them bloody fat ones.

DEAD-CARTER 2

Too lazy to live if you ask me.

DEAD-CARTER 1

Well it's a tough row to 'oe.

DEAD-CARTER 2

It's a dusty old road.

DEAD-CARTER 1

It's a 'eavy old load.

21

DEAD-CARTER 1
Come on then, drink up. It'll lighten the load and brighten the road.

(They drink and move off through the crowd with the cart, singing "Bring Out Yer Bodies (1)." There's a big hullabaloo. Enter EUWA pursued by GUARD and WATCHMAN. She runs into the center of the crowd. They follow and grab her.)

SCENE 5

EUWA
How many times do I have to tell you. It's a birthmark. I've had it for years. It's not the plague.

WATCHMAN
It <u>is</u> the plague. There's no mistaking it. It's a token.

EUWA
IT IS NOT!

(She pulls away and runs up on onto the platform. Some CITIZENS follow to get a better look. Some believe her, some don't. A small riot ensues, during which EUWA escapes, shielded by some of her friends. GUARD and WATCHMAN chase her out of THE SQUARE. CITIZENS and OFFICIALS beckon AUDIENCE to follow and all leave THE SQUARE. THE MUSICIANS are playing in the distance. As they approach the street outside the DUNN'S house. OFFICIALS

and CITIZENS seat AUDIENCE on risers affording them a view of the DUNN'S house, while singing and dancing Blotch (1).

Blotch 1
(Song)

CITIZENS

Mark, there's a blotch, a blaze, a spot
a beauty mark on a beauty. Mark…(Repeat in counterpoint)

CITIZENS & DUNNS

It's not a blotch, it's a bruise,
not a spot, just a bit of pox.
It's not a blain, mister, it's a blister from a burn,
not a carbuncle,
but a bump she's had from birth…(*Repeat in counterpoint*)

CITIZENS

Shut up the house
Paint on the cross.
Lord have mercy
on her soul.
Set two watchmen
at the door
one by day
and one by night…(*Repeat in counterpoint*)

Hey put us away
lock us up so we can die together.
All the gentle folk have gently flown away.
It's a poor's plague, a plague on the poor
In Lon-don-don-don, dondondon-don- don, don-don-don…

(*Repeat in counterpoint*)

(*EUWA enters into the thick of the dance. She has so far eluded her pursuers.*)

EUWA

It's not a token of the plague.
It's a splotch. It is a beauty mark.

It's no buboe, Gawd knows, it's a cross I've born from birth.
It's my disgrace, the flag that flogs my face.

It's a cut, it's not a mark, it's not a spot,
not a sign that I'm dyin' or diseased.
It's a cat scratch that got some dirt caught in it.
It's a scar from a fall 'gainst the handle of a door.

(Enter GUARD and WATCHMAN with the DOCTOR. WATCHMAN and GUARD grab EUWA brandishing their pikes at those who would interfere.)

Is This the House?

DOCTOR
Is this the house?

WATCHMAN (*in unison with CITIZENS and GUARD*)
YES it is   it is   it is   YES it is   it is   it is   the house!

CITIZENS
NO it isn't   it isn't   it isn't   NO   it isn't it isn't it isn't the house!

GUARD
WOT is it?   Wot is it?   WOT is it?   is it   the house?

DOCTOR
This IS the house!

WATCHMAN (*in unison with CITIZENS and GUARD*)
YES   it is   it is   it is   YES   it is   it is   it is   the house!

CITIZENS
NO   it is n't it is n't it isn't NO   it is n't it is n't it is n't   the house!

GUARD
it is   it isn't it is   it isn't it is.   is n't this the house?

DOCTOR
THIS   HOUSE is...

DOCTOR
Indeeeeeeeeeeeeeeeeeeeeeeeeeeeeeeeeeeeeeeeeeeeeeeeeeeeeeeeeeeeeeeeed

DOCTOR, WATCHMAN, CITIZENS & GUARD
in fec ted by the PLAGUE

EUWA

Not.

GUARD & WATCHMAN

Yes it is.

CROWD & EUWA

Not.

GUARD & WATCHMAN

Yes it is.

CROWD/EUWA/DUNNS

NOT!

GUARD & WATCHMAN

Yes it is.

CROWD/EUWA/DUNNS

NOT!

ALL
INFECTED BY THE PLAGUE!

GUARD and WATCHMAN (in unison with CROWD & DUNNS)

Shut it up, Shut it up, Shut it up, Shut it up, (Repeat to fade)

CROWD & DUNNS

You shut up, shut up, shut up, shut up, shut up (Repeat to fade)

27

(GUARD and WATCHMAN throw her in the house as she struggles and, with the help of some CITIZENS, push the DUNNS in behind her. The house is boarded up. A red cross is painted on the front door with the words, "Lord have mercy on their souls." The DUNNS appear at the upstairs window of their house looking out with concern at the crowd as their house is being boarded up. Enter MORT dripping wet with two huge buboes sticking out below his ears on either side. He is obviously in high fever.)

SCENE 6

MORT

Has someone got it? Is the house stricken in there?

CITIZEN

Watch it mate! What are ya doin' out and about? You're endangerin' the lot of us. Don't you realize that, you stupid sod?

MORT

Well I tried to drown meself, but then I remembered I couldn't swim.

CITIZEN

Well, don't you 'ave an 'ouse, a family?

(In the window DUNN waves to MORT. MORT gives him a signal to shut up.)

MORT

Uh....yes…they're up there (*points to DUNNS in the window then realizes his mistake*)…uh… in heaven. They're GUH...gone..

CITIZENS

Well…don't get too close. It's to the pest-house with you.

(GUARD approaches MORT, gives him the once over and cocks his head as
if asking MORT to follow. EUWA calls out from the window.)

EUWA

Don't take that man. He's me man. Morton, is that you? Answer me Mort, how are you?

MORT

I've never seen her before. Her brains are addled by the fever. To the pest-house.

EUWA

Mort! Oh my goodness. Come on up.

MORT

But if they shut me up with you …you'll all get it too, and then we'll all go to the Pit.

CITIZEN

Don't try to protect her mate, she's got it too.

EUWA

I do not!

(WELDON appears in the window.)

WELDON

That man is off 'is nut. He's a public menace. Take him to the pest-house!

WILLIE

GRAND-DAD!

WELDON

He'll be the death of us, I'm tellin' you.

(MUMM appears at the window.)

MUMM

Come on up dear. We'll put you to bed and fix you a nice cup of tea. We'll get a doctor to puncture your blains and then you'll be your old self again. We all will.

GUARD

You're one of them. Get on up there. Come on.

(BRIDGET and WILLIE appear at the window as MORT is climbing up the ladder.)

BRIDGET

Mort looks like he's swallowed a hammer.

WILLIE

Mort looks like he's growing bananas.

MUMM

Shut up, you children.

(MUMM pulls WILLIE and BRIDGET away from the window. MORT climbs in the window and DUNN shuts it.)

GUARD

All right, the rest of you go home. Those of you with no place to go…the Lord Mayor in his wisdom and charity provided a waiting house for those visitors to the city who have their Certificates of Health. Come on now, there's a curfew.

HOMELESS CITIZEN

What about me? I've got no certificate and nowhere to go.

GUARD

To the Pit with you then. There's a terrible shortage of diggers and you'll be paid and fed and put up in a tent Otherwise it's the pest-house. Come on. Get going.

(The HOMELESS CITIZEN leaves as GUARD and OFFICIALS usher
AUDIENCE around the corner of the house to bleachers that afford them a
view of the whole two-story interior of the DUNN'S HOUSE.)

GUARD

All right. This is it. The Lord Mayor apologizes for the fact that he cannot afford you a roof as well as a place to lie on …but all shelters have been requisitioned by the pest-house. If you fall sick in the night, please to report it to this man, (He singles out an OFFICIAL), and he'll take you round the pest-house.

(Inside the DUNN'S HOUSE the DOCTOR is lancing MORT'S buboes. He
is tied to the bed. The whole family is watching.)

MORT

WHAAAAAAAA! YUUUUUUUUUUUH! OOOOOOOOH!

DOCTOR

Just one more little slice and we'll have them both drained.

MORT

YIIIIIIIEEEEEEEEOOOOOOWWWWWW!

(MORT passes out.)

DOCTOR

That's a good sign when the bile suppurates. He might do very well.

DUNNS

Might?

DOCTOR

Might. Might not. There's no telling with this distemper. Now, let's have a look at you.

(EUWA steps forward. He undoes the top of her bodice.)

DOCTOR

Lord have mercy. You've got the tokens.

MUMM

The tokens!

EUWA

Ha, no. It's from the pox I had two years ago.

DOCTOR

I've seen hundreds like you. It's the tokens.

DUNN

And…

DOCTOR

Maybe five or six hours.

MUMM

And…

DOCTOR

Well…say your prayers.

33

DUNN

Oh.

EUWA

What a bunch of rubbish!

WELDON

I've had the plague five times and I've lived through it.

MUMM

Hush. Is there no cure?

DOCTOR

A cure?

WELDON

Yes, a cure, you dimwit.

DOCTOR

Not really.

MUMM

Oh.

DC

But...

MUMM

But what?

34

DOCTOR

I have a little remedy of mine…

MUMM

Yes?

DOCTOR

…for only five shillings.

Only Five Shillings (recitative)

DUNNS

Only five shillings

Only five shillings

Only five shillings

(They give the DOCTOR money.)

DOCTOR

And it sometimes

DUNNS

sometimes

sometimes

sometimes

DOCTOR

works (very well) , BUT…

                    DUNNS
BUT WOT?

                    BUT WOT?

                                        BUT WOT?

                    DOCTOR
It sometimes

                    DUNNS
sometimes

               sometimes

                              sometimes

          DOCTOR *(in unison with DUNNS)*
don't!…   often…   rarely…   hardly…   barely… scarcely

                    DUNNS
     don'tdon't… don'tdon't… don'tdon't… don'tdon't… don'tdon't

                    DOCTOR
…WORKS AT ALL!

(They take the money back.)

                    DOCTOR
BUT…

                    DUNNS
But wot?

          But wot?

                         But wot?

36

DOCTOR

It sometimes

DUNNS

sometimes

           sometimes

                      sometimes

DOCTOR

DO!

(DOC snatches back the money)

DOCTOR *(in unison with DUNNS)*
Some scabious, Pimpernel, Angelica and Rue, Ivy berries, Balm,

DUNNS

do-do   do-do   do-do   do-do   do-do   do-do

DOCTOR *(in unison with DUNNS)*
and Gold boiled in broth and then brewed…

DUNNS

do-do   do-do   do-do   do-do

DOCTOR

…might see her through, but…

DOCTOR

BUT…

DUNNS

But wot?

But wot?

But wot?

DOCTOR

It might cook her goose.

(Pause. All transition into double time. Money goes back and forth as DOCTOR makes it out of the window while the DUNNS argue.)

DOCTOR *(in unison with DUNNS)*

Might see her through, might cook her goose, might see her through (*repeat to fade*)

DUNNS

But it might cook her goose, but it might see her thru, but it might cook (*repeat to fade.*)

DOCTOR

Might COOK HER GOOSE!

(DOC descends the ladder removes it from the window and calls up to the DUNNS.)

DOCTOR

Drink it up in a tea…and you'll be fine. If there are any deaths, don't linger over burial. Cheerio.

(WELDON throws something at DOC as DOC skips happily away with the money.)

WELDON

Little ponce of a charlatan. CHARLATAN!

WELDON & EUWA

We've got to do something.

WELDON

I say we should…

MORT

Water, Waaaahter, I'm burning up.

WELDON

…leave the city and make our way to the outer regions.

MUMM

But we're locked in…for forty days and forty nights dearie. Have you forgotten?

WELDON

They can't hold us. I know a million tricks…I've lived through five plagues and…

EUWA

What about Mort?

WELDON

You might think I'm a bastard to say, leave him. And leave off touching him…and then touching me. He'll not make it. He doesn't have the backbone to live through this. Go say goodbye and pack up…and…

EUWA

SHUT UP DAD!

MUMM

SHUT UP. DAD! We won't die.

DUNN

That's it.

EUWA

Yes.

WILLIE & BRIDGET

Spots. Spots. Who's got the spots? They've got em. I've got 'em, everybody's got the spots.

DUNN

Not me.

MORT

Oh Gawd…oh…

EUWA

He's coming back.

DUNN

Some say there's no need for precaution, that it's the certain end for all time for all of us.

WELDON

Bunch of bloomin' twaddle. The end of the world was supposed to happen yesterday. Some'ow I missed it. But be it by flood or locusts or fire or this bleedin' plague, there's only one way to find out.

EUWA

Wot's that?

WELDON

To stay alive and see.

(WILLIE and BRIDGET are over by MORT's bed, looking at his distended neck.)

MUMM

With Gawd's will we'll all do well.

DUNN

If it were Gawd's will to do us well, he'd kill us now. For we'd be better off in hell than shut up in this house. We've got to get out.

EUWA

Not without him.

WILLIE

That's a walnut.

BRIDGET

No, it's a plum.

WELDON

Get away from him. And don't touch me. Don't touch anyone.

WILLIE

Gramp's got the grumps.

BRIDGET

He's afraid to die.

WILLIE

He's old, that's why.

BRIDGET

And he knows where he'll go.

EUWA

Hush. We won't die.

(EUWA hugs WILLIE and strokes MORT's head.)

EUWA

It's touch that heals. It's fear that tears us apart

WELDON

Before I ride the death-cart I'll be singing a dirge for us all.

DUNN

I don't mind.

MUMM

What?

DUNN

It'd be a good rest y'know. From all o'this. Just shut yer eyes and off yer goes.

WELDON

Who's this?

SCENE 7

(WATCHMAN, GUARD and NURSE, having climbed up the ladder.)

Song of the Nurse and the Watchman

WATCHMAN, GUARD & NURSE

I'm/He's the Watchman by day.
He's the Watchman by night.
I'm/That's the Nurse who stay with you
for forty days and forty nights.

I'm/He's the Watchman by day.
He's the Watchman by night.
I'm/That's the Nurse who stay with you
And care for you until you die.

Forty long days, forty long nights of quarantine.
We'll be together like a family.

WATCHMAN & GUARD

We'll bring your clothes.

NURSE

We'll fetch the food, water too.

WATCHMAN & GUARD

We'll take your slops

NURSE

We'll take everything.

WATCHMAN, GUARD & NURSE

We'll take your dead.
Ded- diddly-dee-ded-diddly-dee, ded, ded
Ded-diddly-dee, ded diddly-dee, ded,
Ded-ded-diddly dee, diddly-dee, ded…(*REPEAT*)

(*The DUNNS huddle mistrustfully and mutter*)

DUNNS

Got to get out of it, got to get out of the town.

Get that cow out of here, got to get out of the town.

(GUARD *takes up his post outside the house. NURSE eyes FAMILY, casing their possessions as WATCHMAN takes note.*)

NURSE

Have no fear of us. We are ready and…table…

WATCHMAN

Table.

NURSE

…to help thee, should thee all become afflicted, as usually happens, thy blood will commence…to pound…

WATCHMAN

Two pounds.

NURSE

We swear to chair…

WATCHMAN

Two chair.

NURSE

…all our aid, for chillings…

WATCHMAN

Four shillings.

NURSE

…and fevers will attack thee. DO not keep thyself up plate…

WATCHMAN

A Plate.

NURSE

…less suspenseful death…

WATCHMAN

Sixpence.

NURSE

rings…

WATCHMAN

Rings.

NURSE

…thy knocker and puts thee in the grounds.

WATCHMAN

Three crowns.

NURSE

Trust us now. We have been through lockups before…

WATCHMAN

Cups.

NURSE

…and with the sick…

WATCHMAN

Six.

NURSE

before. Bob…

WATCHMAN

Bob. Six or four?

NURSE

…and Richard and I, thank Gawds…

WATCHMAN

Tankards.

NURSE

…mercy, that have safely kept us from the fever…

WATCHMAN

A fiver.

NURSE

…when many of our patients , the truth to tell…

WATCHMAN

Total…

NURSE

…have suffered…

WATCHMAN

Four pounds, six and ninepence.

NURSE

...great loss...

WATCHMAN

That they have!

NURSE

And died.

(*A profound silence overtakes the room.*)

NURSE

Well, we must get our rest, musn't we? Watchman, to your post.

(*WATCHMAN exits through the window.*)

NURSE

The rest of ye, to bed. Don't worry. I'll be staying up to see after the sick ones. Go on now.

WELDON

We've got to get rid of this.

MUMM

We'll speak in the morning. Good night, good nurse.

REST

Night, nurse.

(All bed down except the NURSE, who sits up drinking from a gin bottle she brought with her. EUWA scampers behind her to MORT's bed. They whisper.)

EUWA

Mort.

MORT

Whaaaa?

EUWA

Shhh. They've given us a nurse. How are you feeling?

MORT

Uhhh. I don't think I'm long for this world.

EUWA

Shut up with that. Your fever's down.

MORT

I feel like a stuck pig. I don't want to live if everyone else is going to go.

EUWA

That's addled talk. You *must* live.

MORT

Why?

EUWA

I'll be very mad at you if you don't, that's why. I'll kill you if you die.

MORT

Huh-huh-huh. That's funny.

EUWA

Yes. And it wouldn't be funny without you. I need your company. Try. Please?

MORT

Right. Oh Christ.

EUWA

What?

It's just so bleedin' sad.

It's just what happens.

Right.

Song of Feeling

EUWA

Some say it's God's will or Satan's.
Some say it's punishment or a twist of fate.
I don't have the answer or a reason.
All I know is feeling.

Your're put on Earth to feel
the dizzy spin of the turn of the wheel
and in your short circle your heart to reveal.
Your're put on earth to feel

At death's door at birth's gate and life in between
in dreams we have asleep or awake
a cry in the dark, a gasp of fear
a river of joy full of tears.

53

You're put on Earth to feel
the dizzy spin of the turn of the wheel
and in your short circle your heart to reveal.
You're put on earth to feel.

So choose to live or choose to die
to end the play, or pick
another day to dance
to music that you can't predict.

Who can predict the music?

You can only feel.
the dizzy spin of the turn of the wheel
and in your short circle your heart to reveal.
You're put on earth to feel

(This has been MORT's lullaby. He sleeps. EUWA steals a kiss and goes back to her pallet. NURSE, thinking everyone else is asleep, starts filling her bag and bosom with the DUNN's possessions. EUWA sees her, and rouses the house.)

EUWA

She's taking our things.

(NURSE, runs over to EUWA's bed, knocks her down, takes her pillow, puts it over EUWA's face, and sits on it.)

WELDON

Hello, what's up?

(EUWA gets her head out from under.)

EUWA

She's a thief!

NURSE

Its a fever!

(NURSE covers EUWA's face again.)

EUWA

She's killing me.

NURSE

(She continues to smother EUWA.)

WELDON

Why must you make such a ruckus? She's trying to sleep.

EUWA

Mmmmmmmmm. Mmmmmmm.

NURSE

Just a bad dream.

(EUWA overturns NURSE. The DUNNS come pouring downstairs. EUWA and NURSE are fighting and the DUNNS are trying to separate them.)

                                        EUWA
She's a thief.

                                        NURSE
Tie her up.

                                        MORT
Don't you hurt her.

                                        NURSE
Fit o' the fever's got her.

                                        NURSE
Get 'er feet.

                                        WILLIE
Why must you beat her?

                                        NURSE
Bind her.

                                        WELDON
Tie her.

                                        EUWA
Get behind her and blind her.

                                        EUWA

(They sing and fight.)

56

I'm the Nurse I Know What's Best
(Song)

ALL

Often the victims go out of their minds.

NURSE

I'm the nurse, I know what's best.
The fever brings the madness.
The distemper's 'et her mind.
And it's workin' on her insides.
It has sadly touched her nut.
and she can't tell what's what.
You can't believe a thing she says.
'cause she thinks what isn't is.

(Weldon is approaching her with a hammer in his hand.)

I would never harm the hair on the head.
of a poor sick strapping child of a woman
whose dad had a hammer in his hand like yours did.

NURSE

WATCHMAN! WATCHMAN!

FAMILY

She's a hag, a dab, a dross.
She'll have us all on the death cart
then sell our very beds to the next sick sods.
Like a vulture to its feed
she will bleed the ones in need.
The disease it gives her health.

Let's give her cause to nurse herself.

Let's give her cause to curse herself.
Let's stomp her arse and bump her bell.
Let's thump a nail in her pail.
She'll do better off in hell.
Let's stomp her arse…(*repeat*)

(*NURSE is down. WELSON, MORT, EUWA and WILLIE surround her, beat and stomp her in a frenzy. Finally, they stop. She is obviously dead.*)

(*Pause*)

                              WILLIE
Oh – Oh

                               EUWA
Bloody murder.

        (*WATCHMAN calls from below. He's heard something.*)

                            WATCHMAN
Is everything all right?

        WELDON goes upstairs to intercept him. He still has the hammer in his hand.)

                             WELDON
It's the nurse.

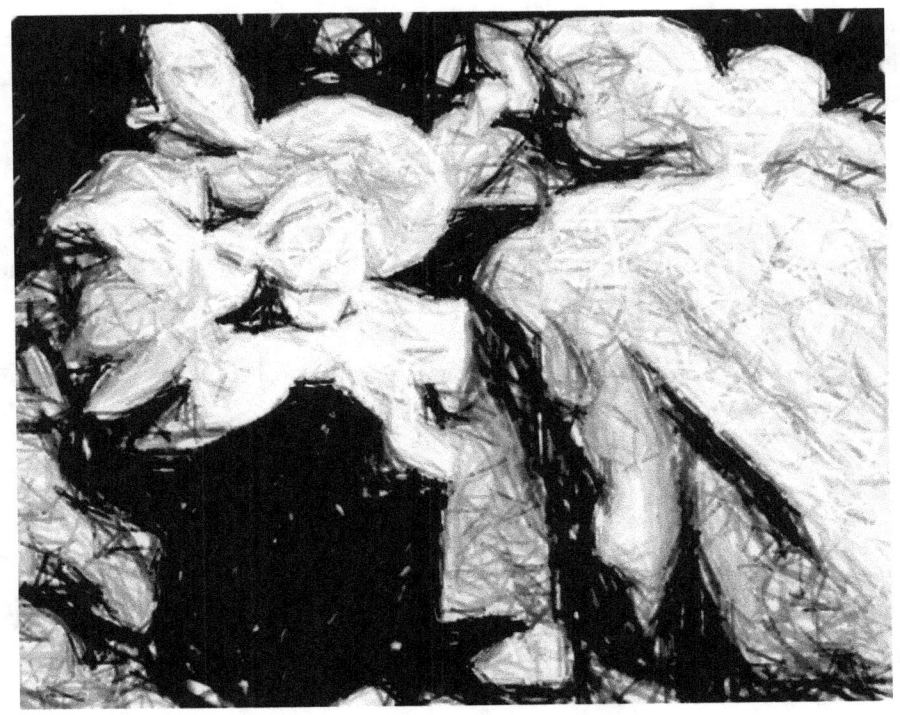

EUWA

She's been taken suddenly very ill.

WILLIE

With the chills.

WELDON

You see, we're covering her up.

WATCHMAN

Well let's have a look at her then.

(FAMILY springs into action, covering up NURSE and shielding her from view with their bodies. WATCHMAN appears in the window and looks down on them from upstairs.)

WELDON *(holding hammer)*

Oh no, you don't want to do that. You see…she overdid it. Good woman spent the entire evening disinfecting our possessions while we were sleeping. Don't bother her. The same thing could happen to you, and we wouldn't want that now, would we?

WATCHMAN:

Yes…I mean…not at all. However, I do need…a little something to pay for some medication for her.

EUWA

Of course you do. Here. Thank you very much for your trouble.

(She throws him a purse of money.)

WATCHMAN

Right, if you need anything…give us a call.

(WATCHMAN exits out the window and resumes his post. WILLIE bounces up and down on the corpse of NURSE.)

WILLIE

Jumpity-jump. Give her the bumps.

EUWA

Get off of it. She's not a plaything.

WILLIE

She's dead. We did it.

EUWA

We had to do it. We had to. Mumm, shouldn't we have a prayer…

MUMM

…for her departed…

WELDON

…thieving carcass?

EUWA

Shut it off, Dad. Mumm.

MUMM

Almighty Gawd.

FAMILY

Almighty Gawd.

MUMM

We had to do it.

FAMILY

We had to.

MUMM

To live.

	FAMILY
To live.	
	MUMM
Let us live.	
	FAMILY
Let us live.	
	MUMM
Forgive us.	
	FAMILY
Forgive us.	
	MUMM
Take this…	
	FAMILY
Take this…	
	MUMM
…poor sinner…	
	FAMILY
…poor sinner…	
	MUMM
…to her just reward…	

FAMILY

…to her just reward…

WELDON

…the nest of dung where she was born.

FAMILY

Amen.

MUMM

Have some respect. Amen.

FAMILY

Amen.

EUWA

Gawd, she nearly had me for leavers.

DUNN

We're in for it now.

WELDON

We've got to get out of here now.

MUMM

But the door's locked and the windows watched.

EUWA

But they've got to open the door for the dead, mustn't they. They can't leave 'em in the houses.

WELDON

Right, so paint up the old doss-bag with spots. And call for the lummox to unbar the door.
Pop him on the head and then bugger off. Euwa, get your paints.

DUNN

Right, Mort, can you walk, lad?

MORT

I can try.

(WILLIE and EUWA paint NURSE grotesquely. MUMM starts tying things
up in a bundle.)

WELDON

Leave it. It's got the plague on it.

(He scratches himself.)

WELDON

Damn fleas. They're everywhere.

MORT

Look at her. Like a harlequin.

EUWA

More like a harlot queen.

WELDON

Call for the Watchman.

(WILLIE calls out the window.)

WATCHMAN

What is it now?

(WELDON goes to the window.)

WELDON

It's the nurse. She died.

WILLIE

And now she's dead.

WELDON

And she's stinkin' the place up.

WILLIE

She's swooooolen.

WELDON

She's too big for the window. Open the door and put her body out for the wagon men.

WATCHMAN

That's too bad. Give us a minute to pry it open, will ya'?

(They pull NURSE's body to the door and wait as WATCHMAN pries the door open.)

The Watchman's Call

DUNN/MORT: Watch man •   Watch man •.   Watch man •   Watch man. •   Watch man •   Watch

MUMM/EUWA: Watch •.   man Watch •   man   Watch •.   man Watch •   man Watch •   man Watch

WELDON/KIDS: •   Watch man •   Watch   man   •   Watch man •.   Watch man •   Watch man   •

DUNN/MORT: man •   Watch man •.   Watch man •   Watch man •   Watch man •   Watch man

MUMM/EUWA: man Watch •   man Watch •   man   Watch •   man Watch •   man Watch •   man

WELDON/KIDS: Watch man •   Watch   man •   Watch man •.   Watch man •   Watch man. •   Watch

DUNN/MORT: •   O   pen • •   up   the •   Doh •   oh   oh   oh   ooooooooooor

MUMM/EUWA: Open •   O   pen   up   the •   Doh oh •   ohoh •   ohoh •   ohoh ooor

WELDON/KIDS: O   pen •   up   the •   Doh •   ohoh •   oh   ohoh ohoh ohoh oooooor

DUNN/MORT: •   Here's a   bod   eee   for   the   dead •   cart •   Here's a   bod   eee   for

MUMM/EUWA: Here's a   bod   eee   for   the   dead •   cart •   Here's a   bod   eee   for   the

WELDON/KIDS: • •   Here's a   bod   eee   for   the   dead •   cart •   Here's. a   bod   eee

DUNN/MORT: the   dead •   cart •   Get   her   out • •   She's start   ed   to   smell •

MUMM/EUWA: dead •   cart •   Get   her   out • •   She's start   ed   to   smell • •

WELDON/KIDS: Get   her   out • •   She's start ed   to   smell • •   Get   her   out she's

DUNN/MORT: •   Get   her   out   •   •   She's start ed   to   swellllllllllllllllllllllllllllllllllllllllllllllllll

MUMM/EUWA: dead   •   cart   •   Get her out   •   •   She's start   ed   to   swellllllllllllllllllllllllll

WELDON/KIDS: start ed   to   swellllllllllllllllllllllllllllllllllllllllllllllllllllllllllllllllllllllll

(WATCHMAN gets the door open and with a hook and gloves, dumps
NURSE's body on on the street. The DUNNS come into the street
surrounding WATCHMAN as WELDON stands by with his hammer.)

WELDON

Watchman?

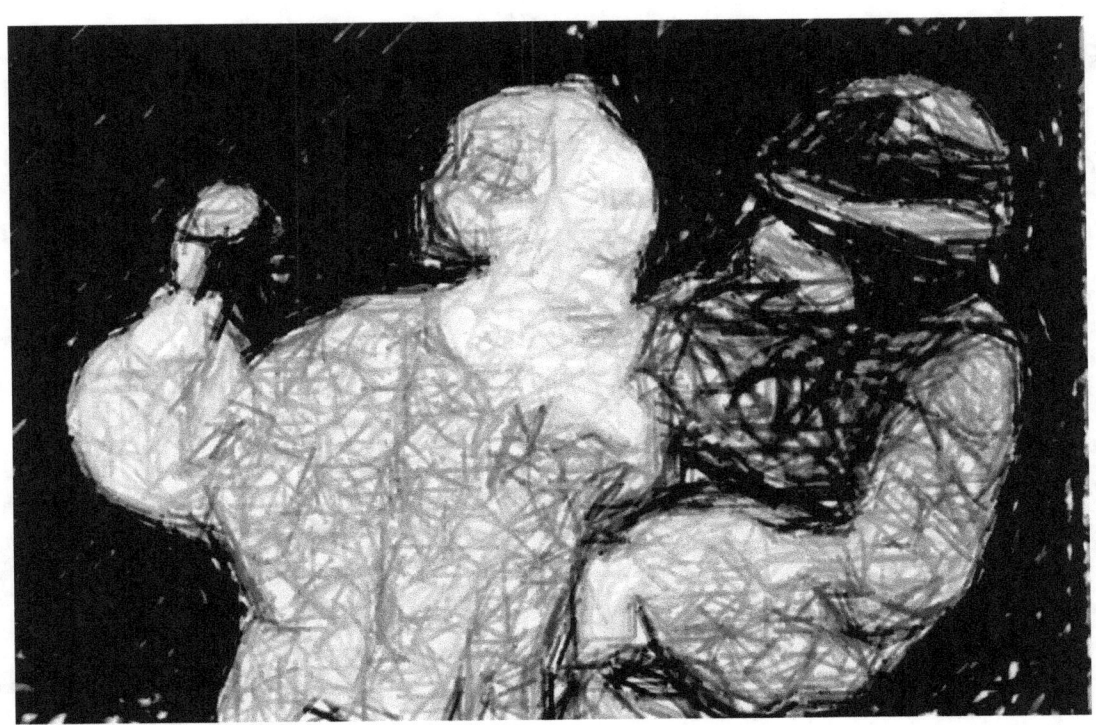

WATCHMAN

Wot man?

MORT

Watch out, Watchman.

WATCHMAN

For wot, man?

WELDON

For wot you watch, man.

EUWA

Hush man, yer us, man.

WATCHMAN

No, ma'am.

EUWA

Don't you watch, man.

WELDON

Don't you watch, MAN!

WATCHMAN

Well, I have to watch . But I don't see, man. I just watch.

WELDON

Not a see-man, just a watchman?

WATCHMAN

Don't see a thing, man.

EUWA

Well, you might see some things 'round here that I'm sure you'll be interested in. We have no need for them now.

WATCHMAN

Ma'am I will watch for them. Indeed.

MORT

Well, stand your watch, man.

WATCHMAN

I will, man.

EUWA

God bless you, man.

WATCHMAN

I am the watchman.

(He whistles. Some CITIZENS run in and carry off the furniture. The DUNNS steal away into the street. In the distance the FERVENT are approaching, singing "The End Begins Again." The CITIZENS fill the street.)

DUNN

What's that?

WELDON

It's the fanatics. They're pickin' up all that have lost their homes and takin' them all to the Pit to help with the buryin'. They do it every night.

EUWA

Well that's good on them, then.

WELDON

No it's not. Bunch of sodding doom-besotted funereal bastards. Come on. Let's get out of here.

*(More and more CITIZENS fill the street. **This is the place where there can be an intermission. If TOKENS is staged environmentally with AUDIENCE mingled with the cast, and an intermission is chosen, it is very important that none of the actors break character.** The Intermission should be short and taken up with the improvisations of the CITIZENS, MUSICIANS and OFFICIALS. They can sell remedies, help each other, play dice, etc. The DUNNS are in the crowd throughout.)*

(If no intermission, continue with SCENE 8.)

SCENE 8

(DOLPHIN appears in the crowd surrounded by the FERVENT with their coffins. They are singing "The End Begins Again," beckoning AUDIENCE to follow them. AUDIENCE moves with them as they sing, from the street outside the DUNN'S house to the street on the way to THE PIT.)

The End Begins Again
(Song)

FERVENT/CITIZENS
And so the end begins, the end begins again.
Until again begins the end begins, and then…
the end ends. And life begins again.
Until the end begins again. And then the end ends.

(REPEAT under the following dialogue)

FERVENT/CITIZENS
The end comes, the end comes, the end comes…*(Repeat under dialogue.)*

FERVENT/ CITIZENS
And again, and again, and again, and again…*(Repeat under dialogue.)*

FERVENT 1
Can't wait for Glory, mate. Come pray with us. Join us on the riverbank, friend.

FERVENT 2
Lend a hand, friend. There's poor souls unburied yet who need a lift to heaven. Come on.

FERVENT 3
You've fear in your eyes and love in your heart, mate. Don't be scared. Come along. It's a beautiful ride to Glory.

FERVENT 1
Don't believe the doctors, mate. I'm not afraid to touch you. I'll put you on my back. I'll pick you up when you fall and I'll pray for you if you'll do the same for me.

FERVENT 2
What are you standing about for? Follow Dolphin. Come on, pitch in, for the love of Gawd.

(OFFICIALS guide AUDIENCE as the CITIZENS and the DUNNS thread their way to an opening in the street as DOLPHIN begins to preach. AUDIENCE can sit on risers on one side of the street, or stand with the crowd. OFFICIALS help those who wish to be seated.)

The End Begins Again (Part 2)

FERVENT/CITIZENS
And so the end begins, the end begins again.
Until again begins the end begins and then
the end ends. And life begins again.
Until the end begins again, and then the end ends. (*Repeat under DOLPHIN*)

FERVENT/CITIZENS
The end comes, the end comes, the end comes…(*Repeat*))

FERVENT/CITIZENS
And again, and again, and again, and again…(*Repeat*)

DOLPHIN
Now death rides triumphantly on his white horse while hell is broke loose.
People fall like leaves in autumn where they are shaken by a mighty wind.
Never did so many husbands and wives die together.
You that have any tenderness left,
you, that have not quite transformed yourself into beasts and devils,
you, that escape hell,
you, that can with any remorse, behold the dying pale faces of families
stabbed at the heart by these sins of yours,
oh, tremble at the fierce wrath of Gawd that is gone forth against you
and abhor yourselves, ABHOR yourselves, for all your abominations.

The End Begins Again (Weldon's Song)

WELDON

If I hear about "the end" again
I'm gonna get me a shovel and dig right in
and then when the world don't end
I won't have to worry 'bout the end again.

Chorus

FERVENT/CITIZENS

And so "the end" begins, the end begins again. (*Together*)

FERVENT/CITIZENS

The end comes, the end comes, the end comes. (*Together*)

FERVENT/CITIZENS

And again, and again, and again, and again. (*Together*)

WELDON

If you're so sure that this is the end,
why don't you please just do yourself in?
And then when the world don't end,
you won't have to worry 'bout "the end" again.

Chorus

WELDON

Don't tell me about the end again.
Die for your own sins. Let me live.
And I will live until the end.
And I'll know bloody well when the end is then.

(CHORUS sways and moans as they sing below the following dialogue.)

Chorus

DOLPHIN

There is no salvation for the living souls. For the dead there is yet the chance of grace.

WELDON

Donkey's arise!

DOLPHIN

Come to the steaming Pit, to the grave, to see what awaits us. Come, all of you. It is a sermon for the eyes that the soul cannot forget.

WELDON

Jump in it then if you like it so much!

EWA

Shut it Gramps! They're just trying to help.

WELDON

With bollocks!

DOLPHIN

To the Pit!

(The FERVENT pick up their coffin, resume their chant and shuffle-dance on to THE PIT, led by DOLPHIN. WELDON stops AUDIENCE from following.)

WELDON

If you've got half a brain you'll not follow them. They've lost their families and have gone demented. They'll wallow in death until it gets them. That's wot they want. They just can't say they want it, for that's a sin. We're looking for a way out of it. Come on, if all of us bind together we could storm the gate.

(DUNN, while listening to WELDON, discovers to his horror, that the "fleabites" he's been scratching on his arm are buboes which are spreading all over his arm, chest and neck and that a fever is coming on. His horror turns to resignation as he realizes a solution.)

DUNN

WAIT!

WELDON

Wot?

DUNN

I have it.

WELDON

How to break down THE GATE?

DUNN

No, the Tokens. They're upon me now.

(The crowd gasps, then turns instantly silent.)

MUMM

Oh Gawd.

WELDON

Don't touch him.

DUNN

All right, you, move, WATCH OUT! Some of us are infected.

(He walks right into AUDIENCE. OFFICIALS part to let him through. He is looking for something. He spies a patch of dirt on a hillock.)

EUWA

What are you doing, Dad? Come on back, we'll get you through.

(DUNN finds his spot.)

DUNN

Here it is. Get me a shovel. Get me some clothes. Here is where I want it.

MUMM

Wot?

DUNN

GET ME A SHOVEL! GET ME SOME CLOTHES!

WELDON

Do what he says.

No Trouble
(Song)

DUNN: I'll dig me a hole in the ground.
             Get me my warmest clothes.
             Then I will lay me down.

(DUNN is given a shovel. He puts on a coat and starts to dig, singing from his hillock.)

DUNN: I'll be no trouble, no trouble, no trouble, no… *(together but not in unison)*
FAMILY: He'll be no trouble, no trouble, no trouble, no…

DUNN: You won't have to carry me.
FAMILY: We won't have to bury him.

78

DUNN: I'll be waiting patiently.

FAMILY: He's being so kind to his kin.

DUNN: I'll be no trouble, no trouble, no trouble, no… (*together but not in unison*))

FAMILY: He'll be no trouble, no trouble, no trouble, no…

DUNN: Don't dump me down in the fields with just anyone.

FAMILY: We won't dump 'im down in the fields with every old body.

DUNN: I wants a hole of me own.

FAMILY: Dad wants a hole of 'is own.

DUNN: A place where you can go and visit with me.

FAMILY: A place where we can go and visit with him.

DUNN: With my name upon a stone.

FAMILY: With his name upon a stone.

DUNN: Bless me, I must go inside.

FAMILY: Bless him, he must go inside.

DUNN: Death will soon be coming and visiting with me.

FAMILY: Death will soon be coming and visiting with him.

DUNN: We'll have something to decide.

FAMILY: They'll have something to decide.

DUNN: I'll be no trouble, no trouble, no trouble, no... (*together*)

FAMILY: He'll be no trouble, no trouble, no trouble, no...

DUNN: Here I go in my hole in the ground.

FAMILY: Bless him, there he goes in his hole in the ground.

DUNN:	Death will soon be coming round to take me down.
FAMILY:	Death will soon be coming round to take him down.

DUNN:	I'll be no trouble, no trouble, no trouble, no… *(together)*
FAMILY:	He'll be no trouble, no trouble, no trouble, no…

DUNN:	I'll be no trouble, no trouble, no trouble, no… *(together)*
FAMILY:	He'll be no trouble, no trouble, no trouble, no…

DUNN:	I'll be no trouble, no trouble, no trouble, no… *(together)*
FAMILY:	He'll be no trouble, no trouble, no trouble, no…

DUNN:	Trouble…
FAMILY:	Trouble…

(End of Song.)

EUWA

But, Dad, you're not acting ill. Look at you, digging away. What if you don't…um…die?

DUNN

You don't have to act ill to be ill. I'll die. I know I will, and I don't mind. Now, don't get close.

MUMM

But dear…

(DUNN is digging furiously.)

DUNN

You don't want to take me to the Pit, do you? This is so much more easy. And, if you live, you'll know exactly where to find me. That'll be nice for us, won't it?

WELDON

He's right. When you get the tokens like that, all of a sudden, with no bumps and swellings, that's it, you're a goner, I've seen it.

DUNN

That's right. I know. I can feel it on my insides. But it doesn't hurt. Isn't that the luck? So stand back and let me get on with it.

(Pause)

WELDON(Beckoning FAMILY to leave.)

Back off then. So let's get on with it. Goodbye Dunn.

DUNN

WAIT! I don't want to bother you, but there's just one thing.

MUMM

What dear? We'll do anything.

DUNN

Have a dance on me grave.

EUWA

A dance?

DUNN

A dance. Have a dance on me grave. Have a celebration. Have a bloody good time.

EUWA

Oh no…

WELDON

We've got to get out of here. We can't be hangin' round, dancin'.

DUNN

DON'T TELL ME NO AT A TIME LIKE THIS! Promise.

(Dunn gets no response to his request.)

DUNN

PROMISE? MUMM?

Well love, if that's what you want…it'll be no trouble.

WELDON

All right, let's get on with it.

(WELDON grabs the shovel from DUNN and gestures for him to get in the grave. DUNN pulls away.)

83

DUNN

Wait a minute. Aren't you going to wait for me to die before you cover me up? I'm going soon. It won't be long.

WILLIE

Gramps, wait till he's dead to bury him. Otherwise the rats will eat his living face off.

WELDON

They're hardly any rats left. They're dying like flies.

MUMM

They're dying like people. The flies are doing very well. Yes, we'll stay.

EUWA

Come on then, let's bed down next to Dad then.

WELDON

All right. We'll wait out the night here and give him his peace. And then in the morning we'll find our way out. So let's all kip together and get some rest.

(DUNN gets in his hole and sits in it.)

DUNN

Will you then stay up to see me off?

MUMM

Of course, Love.

DUNN

Thank you, my dear. It's such a privilege to go in peace with company.

84

MUMM

Yes, it is, isn't it?

DUNN

Yes it is. Goodbye everyone. Don't come too close.

(The FAMILY says goodbye to DUNN. The CITIZENS toss rags and flowers into his grave, where DUNN sits, smiling ecstatically.)

DUNN

And to all of you I don't know. Goodbye…

WELDON

Right, let's kip in.

(Everyone finds a place to sleep by the hillock. MUMM sits by DUNN's hole. EUWA beds her children down and gets MORT comfortable. WELDON stands watch off in the distance but falls asleep immediately. EUWA nods off, but BRIDGET is still awake. WILLIE begins to come down with a violent onslaught of fever.)

SCENE 9

(WILLIE moans fitfully in his sleep. BRIDGET shakes him, rises and goes over to DUNN's hole. She gazes into it. WILLIE staggers up to join her.)

                              BRIDGET
What will happen to him?

                              WILLIE
His soul will go to heaven.

                              BRIDGET
But what about to *him*?

                              WILLIE
The worms will gnaw his bones.

                              BRIDGET
And then what will happen?

                              WILLIE
A bird will eat the worm.

                              BRIDGET
And then what will happen to the bird?

                              WILLIE
A man will eat the bird.

                              BRIDGET
What about his soul?

                              WILLIE
You can't eat that…that goes off…somewhere…OOOOHHH! Uh…Uh.

(He suffers an intense flash of pain.)

BRIDGET

What's the matter? Oh, I'll get Mama. Ma…

WILLIE

No, don't tell her. She'll get real mad. She'll beat me if I die on her.

BRIDGET

How does it feel?

WILLIE

Like my eyes are meltin'. Like me skin is lifting off a fire.

BRIDGET

That's your soul. It's tryin' to get out. Are you going to leave it go?

WILLIE

I guess so. Look, don't tell Mama. Tell her I'm sleeping. Promise?

BRIDGET

Cross my heart and wish to…

(WILLIE dies. In the distance the dead-cart's bell jangles. Bagpipes blare. BRIDGET runs away. The PIPER enters, reeling and staggering, playing a logy Ayre. They finally collapse on their pipe, moaning as the pipe deflates.)

SCENE 10

(Offstage the DEAD-CARTERS approach singing their call.)

Bring Out Your Bodies: (Dead-Carter's Song)

Bring out your bodies.

Bring out your deh-heh-hed, deh- heh- heh-heh- hed.

(They come into the street hauling a half-full cart.)

DEAD-CARTERS
Bring out yer bodies that in yer houses lie.
For on this night we'll take them for a ride
out to the Plague Pits where fresh departed souls
are thrown into holes.

(DEAD-CARTERS stride up with the cart and pick up a PLANTED CITIZEN who slumps into their arms. They load them onto the cart on top of a big dummy.)

DEAD-CARTER 1
Not so fat as that one. *(Pointing to the dummy.)*

DEAD-CARTER 2
That was a bad one, warn't it? But she's not a feather, this one.

(DEAD-CARTER 1 sees WILLIE and lays his body gently on the cart.)

DEAD-CARTER 1

Not like that little one.

DEAD-CARTER 2

Break your heart, those little ones.

DEAD-CARTER 1

But not your back, like that fat one. I 'ates them fat ones.

DEAD-CARTER 2

You 'ates them for what they ate too much of, and I 'ates the little ones for what they never ate at all.

DEAD CARTER 1

Truth of fact I 'ate them all.

DEAD-CARTER 2

I too.

DEAD-CARTER 1

Truth of fact?

DEAD-CARTER 2

I've nothing against them being alive, but dead, they're a great bother.

DEAD-CARTER 1

Not only to us.

DEAD-CARTER 2

To the public at large.

DEAD-CARTER 1

Well, we must be rid of them. Drink up.

DEAD-CARTERS

PICKLE THE PLAGUE! *(They sing.)*

> Into the Plague Pits are ye bodies thrown.
> And pits no more but now dead mountains grown.
> And when the Pit is full we'll stack them higher
> until the mountains above the town do tower.

(They see the PIPER collapsed on his pipe.)

DEAD-CARTER 1

There's one.

DEAD-CARTER 2

Oooh, a skinny one.

(They drag the PIPER to the cart, the PIPER cradling the pipe.)

DEAD-CARTER 1

Well 'eres a piper piped his last pipe, aye?

DEAD-CARTER 2

That's a fine pipe that that Peter Piper piped.

DEAD-CARTER 1

Well, let's bury the piper and keep the pipe.

(He picks up the pipe and tries to give it a toot.)

DEAD-CARTER 2

But though the piping of a pipe infectious be, an infected piper's pipe could infect thee.

(DEAD-CARTER 1 drops the pipe like it's a hot potato.)

DEAD-CARTER 2

Let's bury the piper and burn his pipe.

DEAD-CARTER 1

But that is not a pipe for smoking there. That is a pipe to play a bonny ayre.

DEAD-CARTER 2

Ha-ha. Good one. Very well…let's bury the piper with their pipe.

DEAD-CARTER 1

Good. We'll lay the pipe right next to his head, and then the dead piper can pipe for the dead.

(They put the PIPER on the cart next to the body of WILLIE, place the pipe in the PIPER's mouth, and sing.)

DEAD-CARTERS

Bring out your freshly dead that died today.
This week alone ten thousand have we taken.
And soon in London, there'll no more bodies be
Except for us, and then ourselves we will bury.

                              DEAD-CARTER 1
Let's pit them now.

                              DEAD-CARTER 2
'Tis easier in truth to pit them than to pity them.

                              DEAD-CARTER 1
Save thy pity for when they pit thee.

                              DEAD-CARTER 2
Aha. I will. Look, the moon has risen full. No!

                              DEAD-CARTER 1
Wot?

                              DEAD-CARTER 2
D'ye see upon the moon some spots?

                              DEAD CARTER1
Yes. D'ye think the moon the Plague has caught?

                              DEAD-CARTER 2
It's a greedy Plague.

          (They drink quickly.)

                              DEAD-CARTER 1
It's a thirsty old Plague.

DEAD-CARTER 2

An insatiable Plague.

DEAD-CARTER 1

Pickle the Plague!

DEAD-CARTER 2

Pickle the Plague.

BOTH

PICKLE THE PLAGUE!

(They sing as they roll on towards the Pit.)

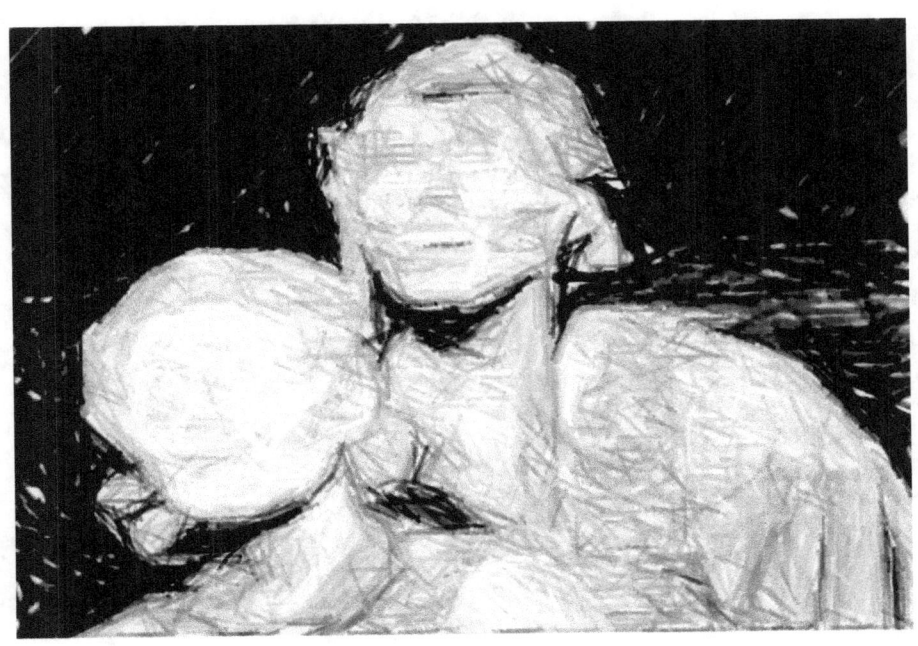

DEAD-CARTERS

Bring out yer bodies that in yer houses lie.
For on this night we'll take them for a ride
out to the Plague Pits where fresh departed souls
are thrown into holes.

SCENE 11

(EUWA, awakened by the singing and rattling of the cart, sees WILLIE's body on the cart. She runs over and grabs his body off the back of the cart, unseen by the DEAD-CARTERS. She holds his body.)

EUWA

Why, Whyeeeeeeee?
Gawd. Gawd took his own son,
Took my only one son.
(To a CITIZEN on the street.)

Why not your son?
Whoreson Gawd. Oh…mercyless, mercyless.

(She sobs. MUMM has heard her and finds her in in the street. EUWA cradles WILLIE in her arms. MUMM leads her back to where they had been sleeping by DUNN's grave.)

EUWA

I couldn't say goodbye.

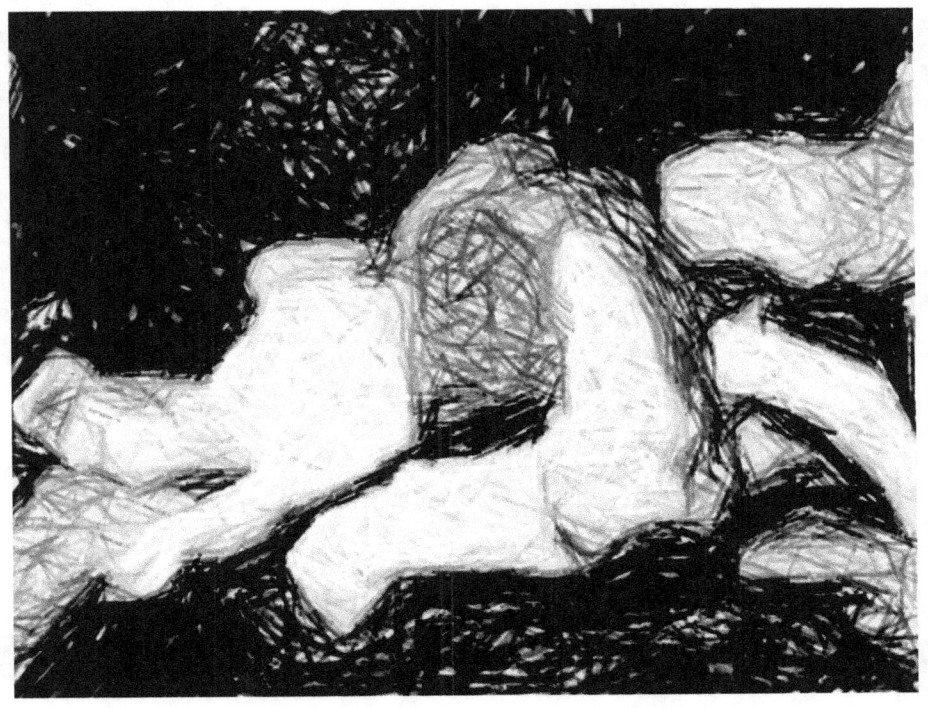

MUMM

You can never really ever.

(MUMM takes EUWA — who is holding WILLIE — in her arms. She sings.)

Come All You Who Fear Forever
(Song)

MUMM

Come all you who fear forever,
fear's a fever, do not feed her.

Death is but your final lover
fearful leaver, last forgetter.

Come and dance with her.
Come and rise.
Rise to fall with the stars in the sky.

While we're on this fateful river
we must sail her, she's to savor.
Life's a favor, do not fail her.
Fear will steal her. Do not waver.

Come and dance with her.
Come and rise.
Rise to fall with the stars in the sky.

MUMM

In a time that's full of horror
live in love, you'll die tomorrow.
Fear's the jailer, be the carer.
'Gainst the terror, be the darer.

Come and dance with her.
Come and rise.
Rise to fall with the stars in the sky.

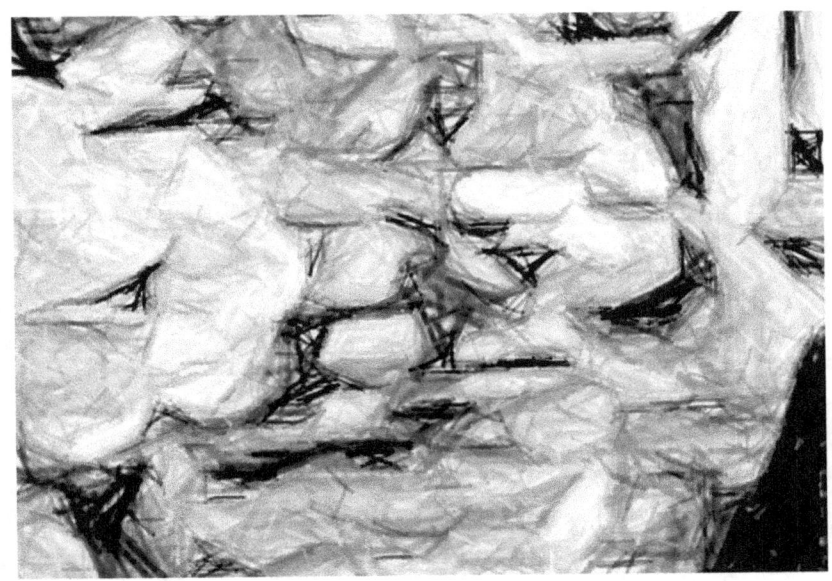

(While MUMM is singing, the atmosphere changes and EUWA, cradling WILLIE in her arms, falls into an hysterical hallucination. The sleeping CITIZENS become the DEAD. WILLIE comes alive and springs out of her arms into the street. She follows him. The DEAD rise and dance, engulfing EUWA. She can't find WILLIE.)

Fever River
(Song)

THE DEAD

Don't be a-fearful.
Feverish lass you will soon pass over
the river of tears.

Death is bloody beautiful.
No one to mourn
there'll be no pain to feel
and nothing to lose.

                    EUWA

Carry me across the water.
Let me find him as he rises from the dead cart.

                THE DEAD

Don't be a-fearful…(*repeat*)

                    EUWA

This is more than just a fever.
I am going now to dance beneath the ghost stars.

                THE DEAD

You're full of fear from the fever river,
fear of the forever.
Be cheerful. What you feel is awful
is something to lose.

            EUWA & THE DEAD

Fever's got me/her in its river.
I'd/She'd be thankful but to lie in cooler waters.

(WILLIE's GHOST dances by EUWA. She tries to catch him, but he eludes her. They play an eerie tag in the ranks of the dancing DEAD.)

THE DEAD
Dance with the Deh-heh-hed
and you will be immortal.
Cast off your dreh-he-hed.
Your fear cannot abort hell.
Kick up your heels to the sky.
Say good bye and die.

THE DEAD
It'd be bloody peaceful.
No one to mourn
there'll be no pain to feel
and nothing to lose.
Kick up your heels to the sky.
Say goodbye and die.

(in ¾ time)

Die die diddly diddly die die
die die diddly diddly diddly dee
die die diddly diddly die die
diddly die diddly dee diddly die

Die diddly die die diddly dee
diddly die die diddly die die
diddly diddly die die diddly
die diddley dee diddley dee

Diddly diddly die die diddly dee,
dee diddly die die diddly diddly
die diddly dee die diddly dee
diddly diddly die die dee,

99

(EUWA finally manages to catch WILLIE. As they touch, the DEAD become shadows.)

Willie/Euwa's Song

WILLIE

Oh Mum, I've gone so far away.
I wandered off alone to play
and found a place where now I stay
where I can't hear you calling.

(PIPER's ghost appears playing between verses)

WILLIE

And have you now come out to see
if I'll be coming home for tea?
You'll look in every ditch for me
to see if your boy's fallen.

EUWA

You fell into a sleep so deep
you'll never wake again from dreams.
And ever more you'll never weep
for no pain will you be feelin'.

WILLIE

And now I'm here to tell you Mum
about the things that are to come.
So listen to your only son
who soon you will be joinin'.

WILLIE & EUWA

Yes, soon we'll be together /Mum/Son.
We'll walk the streets forever, but
we'll never find the home we loved
before we started dying.

We'll never find the home we loved
before we started dying.

(WILLIE collapses. The DEAD and the PIPER's ghost slowly fade into the feverish mist of EUWA's hallucination.)

THE DEAD

Die, die diddly diddly die die…	Die, diddly die die dee…	Diddly diddly die die diddly dee…
…(REPEAT)	…(REPEAT)	…(REPEAT)

(She sits among her sleeping family, holding WILLIE's corpse. It is dawn. The DUNNS awaken.)

EUWA

They're gone.

MUMM

Who's that?

EUWA

They're gone, they're all gone.

MUMM(*Seeing WILLIE in EUWA's arms*).
We must do something with him, Luv.

EUWA

No!

MORT

What's this? Oh no, Euwa… *(He reaches for his son.)*

EUWA

Get away from me!

(She looks at him with hate in her eyes and pulls away, cradling her son.)

MORT

What's to be done with her?

MUMM

Let her keep him. She needs to say goodbye.

SCENE 12:

(MUMM walks over to DUNN's open grave and looks into it. He's dead. She thinks and then wistfully tries out some dance steps. WELDON is awake and watches her incredulously.)

WELDON

Have you gone completely off your nut?

MUMM

It's the promise. Come on. It's time to cover him up. Get up and get on with it.

(MUMM is humming to herself and dancing. WELDON tries to get up, but being quite ill, he has a hard time of it.)

MUMM

What's the matter?

WELDON

I'm all right. It's you I'm worried about.

(He grabs the shovel and starts filling in the hole. MUMM keeps dancing and humming. A MUSICIAN joins her and begins to play the tune for "Spotted Trout." Others hang back tentatively but soon more join in, dancing quietly.)

MUMM

Come on, it's no sacrilege. It's what he wanted.

(More join in. The DEAD-CARTERS wander in without their cart, drunk. DEAD-CARTER 1 is becoming ill.)

DEAD-CARTER 1

Hello…what's this? You can't have a public celebration in such terrible times.

DEAD-CARTER 2

No, you can't. It promotes shameful intercourse between persons, and a shameful lack of attention to the sorrowful work to be done.

DEAD-CARTER 1

Yes, it does. And furthermore, it's against the law.

DEAD-CARTER 2

Yes, it is!

MUMM

Give me that!

(She snatches their bottle and takes a big swig, then grabs DEAD-CARTER 2 and spins him around in a dance.)

MUMM

Dance, damn you!

DEAD-CARTER 1

Well, come on then. Let's have music and a jolly good half hour before the Good Lord in his wisdom sees fit to kill us and squash our spirit once again.

MUMM

DANCE, DAMN YOU!

Spotted Trout
(Song)

MUMM

A spotted trout it leapt so high.
A fish a dah bah dey do.
A spotted trout leapt into the sky.
A fish a dah bah dey do.
And all around the moon did fly.
A fish a dah bah dey do.

Ah what a day to go.
Up in the sky away to go.
Ah what a fate to go.
A fish a dah bah dey do.

(All are joining in by now)

105

It bit the moon and tore it so.
A fish a dah bah dey do.
It bit the moon and swallowed it whole.
A fish a dah bah dey do.
And then the fish began to glow.
A fish a dah bah dey do.
Ah what a day to go...etc.

The speckled trout was in a spot.
A fish a dah bah dey do.
Auld trout's belly got so hot.
A fish a dah bah dey do.
Because the moon begun to rot.
A fish a dah bah dey do.

Ah what a day to go...etc.

The moon got hotter than a coal.
A fish a dah bah dey do.
And in the fish it burnt a hole.
And over London comets did fall.
A fish a dah bah dey do.

Ah what a day to go...etc.

And then its skin it burnt away.
A fish a dah bah dey do.
And then her spots fell from the sky.
Upon us all and now we die...

(Pause)

A fish a dah bah dey do

Ah what a day to go…etc.

(As the CITIZENS and the DEAD-CARTERS dance and sing "A Spotted Trout," another funeral procession of the FERVENT, led by DOLPHIN, comes into the street, singing "The Good Old Way". EUWA, who has been cradling WILLIE and rocking him to the music, immediately joins the FERVENT holding out WILLIE to DOLPHIN as if to say, "Raise him from the dead." DOLPHIN makes a sign over him and takes him from her. EUWA begins to dance ecstatically.

MORT and BRIDGET try to pull EUWA away from the FERVENT, but she shakes them off. WELDON looks on from DUNN's grave despairingly. He is getting sicker by the minute.)

The Good Old Way
(Song)

FERVENT
Lift up your hearts and join us, Friends,
and taste the pleasure friendship lends.
Let nothing cause you to delay
but hasten in The Good Old Way.

For I have the sweet hope of Glory in me soul.
I have the sweet hope of Glory in me soul
and I know I have
I feel I have
the sweet hope of Glory in my soul.

Our conflicts here though great they be
shall not prevent our victory.
If we might strive and hope and pray
like soldiers in the Good Old Way.

For I have the sweet hope of Glory in my soul…etc.

Though Satan may his powers employ
Our happiness for to destroy.
Yet never fear, we'll gain the day
by marching in the Good Old Way.

For I have the sweet hope of Glory in my soul...etc.
And fall we on this mortal shore
we'll meet with those who have gone before
and shout to think we'll gain the day
by marching in The Good Old Way.

For I have the sweet hope of Glory in my soul...etc.

(The two groups become mixed up. In the hearts of the dancing CITIZENS a more "spiritual" feeling takes hold, while the FERVENT, absorbing the joy and carnality of the "The Spotted Trout," lay down their coffins and begin to dance. Back and forth the songs exchange, each verse making converts of the two factions until all are dancing to both songs, tears streaming down their

faces, surprised at the depth of their feelings. The MUSICIANS drive them in a medley of both tunes, faster, faster, ending hysterically, like an ecstatic hoe-down, everyone dripping sweat. At the end of the last bar of the jig. KA-BOOM, the music ends suddenly. Its morning and getting hotter. Both choruses become ventriloquists and begin to secretly buzz.)

ALL

Zzzzzzzzzzzzzzzzzzzzzzzzzzzzzzzzzzzzzzzzzzzzzzzzzzzzzzzzzzzzzzzzz.

DOLPHIN

TO THE PIT! We must bury them before they bloat.

(He lifts up WILLIE.)

DOLPHIN

Glory awaits us.

SCENE 13

(The FERVENT and EUWA start off for THE PIT humming "The Good Old Way", ecstatically. WELDON and MORT feebly try to reach EUWA but are thrown off by the FERVENT's rear guard.)

WELDON

Don't fall in with this lot. They'd just as soon jump in the grave as visit it.

EUWA

Come with us, Gramps.

(EUWA looks back at them, then turns and keeps going.)

WELDON

If we all stick together we could find our way out.

MUMM

If we all stick together we could bury the dead.

CITIZEN 1

Go with you? And him with buboes as big as me bollocks? Not on your life!

CITIZEN 2

Look at the fear frozen on the old one's bonce. He's a sinner, and he's scared of what justice awaits him. *(To WELDON and MORT)* You have no need to fear this infection if you're at peace with Gawd. All London needs our help now that we are so sorely afflicted.

CITIZEN 1

Yes, stay, and for extra fortification before you go do your duty, as an extra precaution, I have a tested remedy that has kept me alive and healthy through the thick of it, for only eight shillings…

(CITIZENS heckle and pummel the shyster. A small riot occurs. GUARD enters, using his pike as a crutch. He is obviously on his last legs.)

GUARD

Break it up!

(GUARD collapses.)

WELDON

Look, if the guard is taken ill, there'll be no stopping us at the gate.

MORT

But what about Euwa?

WELDON

She's made her choice.

GUARD

It's no use trying to escape. All the roads have constables turning back those who are trying to flee the town. They're boilin' the mail from London. They'll be boilin' the people next.

WELDON

Then we'll take to the woods.

GUARD

The woods are full of the likes of you. If they're not dead, they're infected, and if they're not infected, they're half-starved and off their nut.

WELDON

I've been there son. In the Plague of '41...

BRIDGET

Shut it off Gramps, you're only thinkin' of yourself. You'd leave me if I was sick, the same way you're trying to leave my Mum and our Willie.

(*She pulls at his hand to follow EUWA.*)

WELDON

She left *us*! I'm not leavin.'

CITIZEN

She's right. All you've been saying is leavin.'

MUMM

That's right, Dad.

MORT

(*Finally standing up to WELDON.*) Gramps, shut yer bleedin' hole, and *come on*! We can't leave her, so move it! There's nowhere to go but the grave it seems.

CITIZEN

To the Pit then. You'll get to dig in a shovel 'for you dig in your heels.

WELDON

Yes, but if you don't look out for yourself, who will?

CITIZEN

The wagon man will.

(*They set off for THE PIT half dragging/carrying the protesting WELDON.*)

SCENE 14

(OFFICIALS beckon AUDIENCE to follow the rest of the crowd to THE PIT. As they enter, they hear the "Song of the Pit," and see a terrible sight; the FERVENT are dumping the bodies into THE PIT. DOLPHIN is working feverishly. EUWA holds WILLIE. DOLPHIN is working feverishly. The DEAD-CARTERS are standing on a pile of bodies on the dead-cart. DEAD-CARTER 1 is collapsed in DEAD-CARTER 2's arms. Occasionally some of the FERVENT lie down in THE PIT and are covered with other bodies.)

Dump the Cart/ Song for the Pit:

5/4

CITIZENS: Dump   the   cart   and pay your respects (lines sung(together)
FERVENT: Come bear witness   to their   deaths

CITIZENS: Pack them close   leave room for   your self.
FERVENT: Send   a   bless   ing   with   your sweat

CITIZENS: And when the load   is done   go, get another   another
FERVENT: And when your prayer is done   keep on prayin'   prayin'

CITIZENS: And when the   pit is full   dig some more   dig some more
FERVENT: And when your heart is full   let tears fall   let tears fall

CITIZENS: And when   you're dead   and gone   keep diggin'   keep diggin'
FERVENT: And when   you can't   go   on   then remember   remember

4/4

CITIZENS: Here's the tunnel   straight to heaven
FERVENT: See   their souls   arising   rising

CITIZENS: In the ground there is a door
FERVENT: to the sky   their spirits soar

115

CITIZENS:	Dirt and lime is our salvation
FERVENT:	Can you hear them calling, calling?
CITIZENS:	This is your rewaaaaaard
FERVENT:	Come claim your rewaaaaaard
CITIZENS:	This is your rewaaaaaard
FERVENT:	Come claim your rewaaaaaard

DEAD-CARTER 2

Hello, give us a hand.

(DEAD-CARTER 2 holds DEAD-CARTER 1, dead in their arms.)

DEAD-CARTER 2

My collaborator is resting now, plum worn out they are from their considerable labor fillin' holes and emptyin' bo'tles. They'll be on the job in a wink, I'm sure, but until they wakes, and they might not in my lifetime at least, they've leff me short-handed, haven't they? They has. I'd hate that the bumpin' of the cart should give 'em indigestion in their dreams, so who'll help me now move the lummox to a spot that'll stay in one place for a while? Anyone? They lost the bet the stupid sod and didn't pay. COME ON!

(DOLPHIN steps and helps DEAD-CARTER 2 walk DEAD-CARTER 1 to the edge of THE PIT.)

DEAD-CARTER 2

They never walked this well when they was awake.

DOLPHIN

Scoffer. You stink of gin.

DEAD-CARTER 2

You stink of Gawd. At least gin disinfects.

(DOLPHIN, enraged, springs back, leaving DEAD-CARTER 1's body to topple into THE PIT.)

DOLPHIN

You must change your Gawdless ways lest you bring down even worse destruction.

(DOLPHIN holds out his arms to EUWA who is holding WILLIE. She won't give him up.)

DOLPHIN

Look at this. This is Gawd's mercy. Praise him.

FERVENT

Praise him!

DOLPHIN

You cannot take back from Gawd. He lets the dead lie, and the living live.

(MUMM, MORT, WELDON and BRIDGET arrive at THE PIT.)

WELDON

Let him lie then. It's all the same to the dead whether they're buried or not.

MUMM

But it's not all the same to the living.

MORT

You told me to live…to keep trying.

EUWA

So you lived. But he didn't. Why should we live? So Gawd can watch us wriggle on his hook?

MUMM

There are plenty of reasons to live. But only if you live can you see them.

EUWA

I don't want to see them. TAKE HIM GAWD! TAKE US ALL!

(EUWA leaps into THE PIT with WILLIE in her arms. From within the
pile of bodies comes the sound of bagpipes. EUWA, still holding WILLIE,
screams in fear. MORT grabs her and pulls her out of THE PIT.)

CITIZEN

It's BEELZEBUB!

(DEAD-CARTER 2 jumps onto the pile and begins throwing bodies this way
and that.)

DOLPHIN

Hear it! It is the cry of the dead come to haunt thee.

It is their voice bleating in thy ear:

"Because of thee am I consigned to torment.

Because of thee my voice screams in the night…Oh Lord…"

(From the center of the pile emerge the spiney chanters of the bagpipes followed by the head, shoulders and person of the PIPER. The PIPER, whose hair has turned white, clambers on top of the bodies and plays a slow hypnotic wailing aire. The FERVENT are cowering. DOLPHIN is on his knees.)

120

PIPER

Don't be scared. I ain't the Devil. I've seen 'im though. I got gloriously pissed and when I awoke I had the whole bloody world sleepin' in me bed. And a very dead lot they were too. Their cold arms wrapped around me, and they tried to drag me under, but I said, "No, I'm for more lively bedfellows than you. You're no fun at all, if you ask me." So back I came, and here I am.

(No one moves.)

PIPER

And a beautiful day it is, too. The light on the clouds…it's a miracle, aye?

(PIPER sniffs the air.)

PIPER

But the air in this place is like an auld meat pie. So, what are you all, paralyzed?

(PIPER sees EUWA holding WILLIE.)

PIPER

Oh, such a great shame. Well you'll have to let him go, woman. Don't you see, you'll have to get another one. There's plenty without mothers you know. Give him here.

(BRIDGET runs to EUWA. EUWA gives WILLIE's body to the PIPER, who gently lays it down. EUWA's eyes come alive again.)

PIPER

Christ, I've been at hell's door and I'm still game for more of it.

DOLPHIN

Think you a body dies any different outside the town? Stay, help us bury the dead.

MORT

Go blow your horn in a sheep's ear.

MUMM

Go on. Get out of here.

WELDON

Are you not coming?

MUMM

No, there's something to learn from the Dead. Some sermon they preach. I can't leave 'em. They're as much me family as you are now. But you go, now, find a way to live before it's too late.

EUWA

A way to live, yes, yes.

MUMM

Go on. Get out of here.

WELDON

Right, we'll meet when this is done. Goodbye.

(He beckons to the CITIZENS and the DUNNS to follow him, but staggers. MORT tries to prevent his fall and accidently rips WELDON's tunic, revealing tokens on his chest and arms.)

EUWA

Not you too?

WELDON

Two weeks before any of you.

MORT

Why didn't you leave? You stayed and risked us all.

WELDON

I didn't want to die alone.

MORT

You gave it to me. And then you'd have had me in the pest-house.

(Pause)

MORT

Well, come on, I'll give you a hand.

CITIZEN

He's not long for it now.

EUWA

NO!

(She points to THE Pit where MUMM is working with the FERVENT, then points to WELDON.)

EUWA

Go take your place. Lend a hand. Like you told her, we'll meet when this is done.

(*WELDON says 'goodbye' with his eyes.*)

EUWA

The rest of you, come. We don't know what's out there, but it's got to be better.

SCENE 15

(*They leave THE PIT. OFFICIALS beckon AUDIENCE to follow the CITIZENS, gently herding them towards the street outside the DUNN's house. DOLPHIN, the FERVENT, WELDON and MUMM stay, working*

*in THE PIT and then, once AUDIENCE is gone, they blend in with the
CITIZENS, walking behind them to THE GATE. Slowly ALL walk away
from THE PIT, past the street outside the DUNN's house, to THE SQUARE
inside THE GATE. As they walk, some of the CITIZENS drop to the ground.
AUDIENCE is directed to step around them.)*

*(ALL make their way towards music coming from THE SQUARE. Inside
THE GATE the MUSICIANS are playing. The CITIZENS and the DUNNS
arrive at THE SQUARE and mount a platform facing THE GATE.
GUARD, limping on his pike, topples, just as he reaches THE SQUARE.
MORT picks him up and lays him on the platform.)*

*(When the whole CAST and AUDIENCE is assembled EUWA addresses
them.)*

EUWA

Those of you who have a place to go, goodbye. Go on your way. The rest stay with us. Take care of each other. If this is the end, let's do it. With exquisite feeling.

(The FERVENT, DOLPHIN, MUMM and WELDON join the rest of the CAST on the platform.)

ALL

And so the end begins, the end begins again.
Until again begins the end begins and then…
the end ends, and life begins again.
Until the end begins again, and then the end ends.

(They repeat with a faster tempo until it ends. The CAST pauses, then bows.)

REPRISE

(For CURTAIN CALL use "Isn't it Grand Boys" segueing into "Glory in my Soul.")

ALL

Look at the People
bloody great spirits.
Isn't it grand, boys
to be bloody well dead?
Let's not have a sniffle
let's have a bloody good cry

Always remember the longer you live
the sooner you bloody well die.

For I have the sweet hope of Glory in my soul.
I have the sweet hope of Glory in my soul
and I know I have
I feel I have
the sweet hope of Glory in my soul.

*(THE GATE opens and OFFICIALS lead AUDIENCE and the CAST out
into the lobby.)*

FINIS

The Music of TOKENS

The music of TOKENS is extraordinary in many ways. It combines tradition and folk elements into a grand counterpoint that's unique, not only in form and structure, but also in its power to inform and transcend. In all my years of musical life, I've never encountered so ingenious yet largely unconscious an arrangement of patterns such as that conceived by David Schein (especially in the big ensemble pieces, like Fever River and The End Begins Again). At the time I considered David's strange linear notation to be naive, but inspired, and though not originally intended as music, it was soon evident to me that it could be turned into just that, and so I set out to transform the speech-songs of TOKENS into compositions. TOKENS is a musical.

A complete score of TOKENS is available for performance, including charts and arrangements for chorus and soloists as well as for a small group of on-stage musician-actors, with instrumentation, violin(s) sackbut (trombone), penny whistles, Irish harp, and various percussion including snare drum. (Other, or additional instruments can be substituted, as the score is designed for maximum flexibility.) Excerpts from TOKENS, performed by my chorus, Music In the Blood, can be seen and heard on my website: candacenatvigenglish.com

Working on TOKENS and generating the score as a lasting testament to its brilliance and future possibilities, is a crowning achievement of my musical life, and a privilege for which I thank David, and which I shared with the other collaborators: Bob Ernst, John LeFan, Freddie Long. I'd also like to take this opportunity to thank Jon English, TOKENS sackbut player and my life-long musical partner and teacher. He is gone, but his inspiration lives on. And the end begins again….

Love and gratitude to all who know and will discover TOKENS,

—Candace Natvig English, co-composer of TOKENS

About the Author

David wrote TOKENS, and with Candace Natvig English, composed and arranged the music. He is a theater artist, composer, writer and teacher and was a founding member of the Iowa Theater Lab and Berkeley's Blake Street Hawkeyes.. He has performed in pieces by Robert Wilson and the composer Lucanio Berio, toured with Whoopi Goldberg and was a contributing writer to her first Broadway show. He performed his solo piece "Out Comes Butch" in Europe and North America for 35 years. In 2002 Schein founded One Love AIDS/HIV Awareness Theater with a troupe of street youth in Ethiopia. He has created innumerable solo shows, four musicals, many collaborations and has authored two books, "My Murder and Other Local News", performance poems, published by Fomite Press, and a novel, "The Adoption," also published by Fomite. He has taught at Brown University and Naropa and at many schools and colleges including the once marvelous Burlington College. His career as a non-profit manager includes Chicago's Free Street Theater, the Arts Council for Chautauqua Co. (NY), the Willowell Foundation (VT) and the Vermont People with AIDS Coalition. He presently is the Grants and Project Manager for Alnôbawai, a Vermont-based non-profit dedicated to preserving Abenaki indigenous traditions, and lives in his hometown, Burlington, VT with his wife, the actress Dana Block, and his parakeets, Jet Blue and Banana.

More plays from Fomite...

William Damkoehler — *The Occupant* and *Self-Storage*
Stephen Goldberg — *Screwed and Other Plays*
Vincenzo Lamartora/Michael Palma — *Altera Matera/It Was* (dual language Italian/English)
Michele Markarian — *Unborn Children of America*
Hanna Eady and Ed Mast — *The Mulberry Tree* and *The Return*

Writing a review on social media sites for readers will help the progress of independent publishing. To submit a review, go to the book page on any of the sites and follow the links for reviews. Books from independent presses rely on reader-to-reader communications.

For more information or to order any of our books, visit:
http://www.fomitepress.com/our-books.html

www.ingramcontent.com/pod-product-compliance
Lightning Source LLC
Chambersburg PA
CBHW081331120626
46546CB00011B/3295